First Published–2005

ISBN: 81-7141-946-1

Published by:

DISCOVERY PUBLISHING HOUSE

4831/24, Prahlad Street, Ansari Road, Darya Ganj
New Delhi–110 002 (India)
Phone: 23279245, • *Fax:* 91-11-23253475
e-mail: dphtemp@indiatimes.com

Printed at:
Amit Enterprises, Delhi

Preface

The figures sound alarming. The towns and cities in developing countries are growing faster than ever before. By the year 2000, 2.2 billion people will live in the cities of the Third World. Their numbers are expected to double by the year 2025. But many of the cities in Africa, Asia and Latin America are already bursting at the seams. Some of the so-called megacities have more than 10 or 15 million inhabitants. Many of them live in unplanned squatter settlements, without water and electricity, in an environment of squalor, poverty, crime and disease, Nevertheless, the cities seem to have lost nothing of their attraction for the rural populations. Although the larger share of the population increase in the cities of developing countries is caused by the children of people already living there, the rural-urban migration continues unabated. The cities still offer better chances for employment and education, they provide a better physical infrastructure, better health facilities and a more interesting life. Miserable as conditions in the cities often appear to be, they are usually much better than those in the rural areas. It is, therefore, an illusion to believe that the growth of the cities could be checked by concentrating the development efforts on the countryside. There is no alternative to urban development in a world will soon count some 8 billion people.

Cities have always been in the vanguard of development. The ancient civilizations of Mesopotamia, Egypt, Greece and Rome were city cultures which for the first time in human development created large, well-governed states. In Europe during the Middle Ages, the creation of towns and cities offered the rural populations a chance to evade the oppression by feudal authorities and become free citizens. Local self-government in medieval towns is at the cradle of democratic development. There is a clear separation of competences between the national, state and local level of government leaving citizens an opportunity to decide on matters which directly affect their own local environment. It is worth looking at this model when discussing ways organized to improve city governance and allow for more participation of the population.

Another fact worth looking at is the size of cities in Industrialized countries. Although about three-quarters of the people live in urban areas, there are only a handful of really big cities.

Of course, the growth of towns and cities in developed countries is the result of a long historical process, deeply rooted in the particular political and economic conditions of the past centuries. In developing countries today, other conditions prevail which favour the emergence of ever bigger urban conglomerations. However, governments are able, thorough appropriate investment and the location of industries educational facilities, or housing policies to influence the settlement trends in their respective countries in favour of smaller cities.

Dr. M. Lakshmi Narasaiah

Contents

1 Towards Healthy Cities

More than a third of the urban population in developing world live in housing of such poor quality with such inadequate provision for water, sanitation, drainage, garbage collection and health care that their health is constantly under threat. But, properly planned, cities can be safe and healthy.

In the cities of India, it is common for one child in three to die before the age of five and for virtually all infants, children and adults who survive to have disease burdens many times higher than they should.

Diarrhoea, tuberculosis and respiratory infections (each among the largest causes of death) are generally much increased by over-crowding. Many accidental injuries happen when there are three or more persons living in each small room in shelters made of flammable materials and there is little chance of providing occupants (especially children) with protection from open fires or stoves.

But cities also include some of the India's safest and most healthy neighbourhoods. High densities allow much lower costs for supplying each household with piped, treated water supplies and most forms of health, educational and emergency services.

Sanitation and drainage may be costly in cities, as complex systems are needed to cope with high densities and large population concentrations but city households can generally afford to pay more—and are prepared to do so if they get a good service.

Cities may be considered ecologically unsustainable because of high consumption and waste levels but well planned and managed cities can combine high living standards with remarkably low levels of energy consumption, resource use and wastes. The concentration of people and production creates many more possibilities of collecting and recycling wastes and for walking, bicycling and a high quality public transport.

For many, city-life is one of excessive workloads and drudgery, yet cities remain centres of culture—including the visual and decorative arts, music, dance, theatre and literature. Most cities have a large reserve of young people on whose initiative and energy they could draw to improve condition—yet most such people find that their cities offer them little hope and little prospect of employment. If cities have such potential to provide healthy, stimulating and valued places to live and work for all age groups, why do so achieve this?

Supporting Change

Much of the explanation is the lack of 'good governance'. Good governance in any city means encouragement and support from all levels of government for a great range of investments of capital, expertise and time by individuals, households, communities, voluntary organisations and NGOs—as well as private enterprises. In most cities in India, the total value of investments made by people in their own homes and neighbourhoods exceeds many times the total value of capital investments made by city and municipal authorities. Yet governments and aid agencies usually ignore (or deem illegal) most such efforts.

Most households who want their own home cannot afford to purchase one—or at least one that is legal. They cannot obtain housing loans so the cost of the house purchase can be spread over a number of years—as they cannot meet the (usually) inappropriate conditions set by banks or housing finance institutions. If they turn to building their own home-as most do—they have to occupy or purchase the site illegally. They often have to build on dangerous sites—in floodplains or on slopes with frequent landslides or mudslides—as the cost of safer sites is too high.

Even if they can qualify, for a housing loan; most such loans are for finished houses, not for incremental construction.

And even when they have developed their own home and neighbourhood into a viable residential area, governments usually refuse to provide these with roads, water supplies, drains and other essential infrastructure, because they are 'illegal'

What would cities look like today if governments had supported these individual and community efforts by ensuring that land, building materials, credit and technical advice were as cheap and readily available as possible? Or if government-community partnerships had been formed to, at least, improve water supply, sanitation, drainage and health care.

These work within what is often called the 'social economy'—the great variety of initiatives and actions that are organized and controlled locally and that are not profit-oriented. The social economy includes the work of citizen groups, resident's associations, street or barrio clubs, youth clubs, and parent associations that support local schools. It includes many voluntary groups that provide services for the elderly, the physically disabled or other individuals in need of social. It often includes many initiatives that make cities safer and more fun helping provide supervised play space, sport and recreational opportunities for children and youth. It may provide formal or informal supervision or maintenance of parks, squares, and other public spaces.

The social economy not only 'gets things done' but also creates a dense fabric of relationships that allows citizens to work together in identifying and acting on local problems. Its value to a 'healthy city' is enormous, even if it is often forgotten by governments and international agencies.

The capacity of city authorities to govern is not the same as the capacity to invest, since these authorities can do much to encourage and support the social economy. City authorities can often greatly increase the supply and reduce the cost of land for housing by changing inappropriate regulations, streamlining planning and land use control, procedure and making better use of publicly owned land.

City authorities should also have the main role in enforcing legislation on, air and water pollution and occupational health and safety. This does not require large investments by public authorities, but it can do much to improve health and the quality of life in a city. Good governance also means managing competing claims and finding common ground between enterprises, trade unions and residents about what should be done to make the city more healthy.

Achieving a healthy city needs a representative political system through which the priorities of citizens and businesses can influence policies and actions. Democratic structures remain among the best checks on the misallocation of resources by city and municipal governments. Actively involving a wide range of local groups in developing 'city governance' helps ensure that the different priorities of a wide range of groups are addressed.

The key issue is not so much identifying what should be done to achieve more healthy cities. This is well known. It is identifying how it should be done, especially how governments and international agencies can support a vast range of activities by individuals, households and communities that help build and maintain healthy cities—which to date they have ignored or even (for many governments) repressed.

Sustainable Cities 2

Today almost one half of the world's population lives in cities. The world's cities are growing by one million people each week. Cities today play a significant role in development. They continue to attract migrants from rural areas because they enable people to advance socially and economically. Cities offer significant economies of scale in the provision of jobs, housing and services, and are important centres of productivity and social development.

However, the stress of this rapid urban population growth is often overwhelming. The long list of afflictions includes urban poverty rates of up to 60 per cent. Despite growing investments, more than one third of the urban population live in substandard housing. Forty per cent of urban dwellers do not have access to safe drinking water or adequate sanitation. Primarily due to a rapid growth and a deteriorating urban environment, at least 600 million people in human settlements (cities, towns and villages) already live in health-and life-threatening situations, and almost 50 per cent of these are children.

The high rate of urban population growth in most regions has led to common problems: congestion, lack of funds to provide basic services, a shortage of adequate housing and declining infrastructure, to name a few.

While these problems are occurring in urban areas, cities still have an important role to play in protecting the global environment in the face of rapid urban population growth. Agricultural and livestock production in rural areas are pushing farther and farther into ecologically fragile regions and cannot support growing population. The finite land and water resources make it imperative that human settlements be carefully planned.

Indeed, sustainable urbanisation will ease the pressures caused by encroachment on fragile natural habitats.

India's cities offer a bewildering sight to any visitor: the congestion caused by rapid population growth and a continuing rural-urban drift often leads to conditions which defy all rules of orders, hygiene and environmental safety. Inadequate leadership, corruption and mismanagement have a harmful effect on the physical, environmental, social and ethical structures of cities in India.

Millions of people live in inadequate conditions—without piped water, electricity, security of land tenure, access to roads or health facilities. The means available for production and financing of housing and urban infrastructure are too limited to meet basic needs.

Reducing Poverty and Creating Jobs

Urban poverty is rising at an alarming pace, especially among women. The informal economic sector—which makes a substantial contribution to the delivery of services, production of goods, building of infrastructure and housing construction—often provides the only opportunity for the urban poor to make a living.

Local informal housing construction, for example, generates up to 20 per cent more jobs than high-cost construction. Street hawking, waste recycling and food production are primary sources of income among the urban poor and are illustrative of the creativity of survival strategies.

However, the informal sector itself is often highly exploitative and fails to raise people's economic development beyond mere subsistence. Larger economic strategies and more participatory urban planning approaches that take stock of local skills, technologies and materials are required to generate new and better-paying job opportunities in cities and towns.

Incorporating Environmental Concerns

In 1992 the Rio Conference on Environment and Development designed the Agenda 21 Programme of Action to help save a planet endangered by environmental neglect and plagued by poverty and underdevelopment. Most of the goals agreed to in Rio can become reality only through local action in cities where environmental threats are increasing. Again, it is the urban poor who are particularly endangered by environmental degradation and pollution. The world's Agenda 21 will fail if the city's environmental agenda (population, inadequate sanitation, water supply and waste management) is not addressed. This is being recognized by local authorities all over the world.

Sustainable development in the twenty first century will to a large degree, depend upon how cities, towns and villages everywhere interact with the environment and utilize natural resources.

Increasing Awareness of Gender issues

Women and men use and experience cities differently, according to their roles, responsibilities and access to resources. For example, when basic services are lacking in a settlement, more often than not it is women who take on responsibilities such as water collection and refuse disposal. Women often have unequal access to resources such as property, credit, training and technology. All of these factors must be addressed urgently, as they make it harder for women to improve their living standards and those of their children.

Disaster Mitigation Relief and Reconstruction

As cities become large and more densely populated, they become increasingly vulnerable to natural and man-made disasters such as earthquake, floods, industrial hazards, epidemics, civil strife and wars. Poor people are forced to live in the most exposed, dangerous and cramped conditions; in flood-prone areas, on steep hillsides or near polluted streams and waste dumps. As a result, they are most likely to lose their homes or their lives when disasters occur. Better planning, access to affordable urban land, and improved construction methods can reduce the extent of catastrophes.

These successful and sustainable approaches to poverty eradication; managing the urban environment; providing access to land, shelter and finance; empowering women and men; and many other issues will have to be documented and disseminated widely.

Cities at the Forefront 3

The rapid growth of cities in the developing world puts them in the forefront of the struggle for improved living standard and protection of the environment. Since 1950 the urban population has more than tripled, from just over 750 million to about 3 billion. By 2030 some 5 billion people will live in cities. In the developing world the urban population is projected to double from 1.9 billion in 2000 to be just under 4 billion by 2030.

Worldwide, about three fourths of all current population growth is urban. Cities are gaining an estimated 55 million people per year—over 1 million new residents every week from in-migration and natural population increase within cities. In developing countries many cities are growing two or three times faster than population growth for the country as a whole. As cities grow ever lager, their impact on the environment grows exponentially.

The Rise of Megacities

The UN coined the term megacities in 1970s to describe cities with 10 million or more residents. As recently as 1975 there were only five megacities worldwide. Currently, there are 19 megacities, of which 15 are in developing countries. By 2015 the number of megacities will grow to 23 which is explained in Table 3.1. Megacities have captured public interest because cities this large are unprecedented in history and because of the popular perception that human well-being will decline in such dense concentration of people.

Millions of people move from the countryside to the city to seek a better life, but they often find that their lives become more difficult. In many cities 25% to 30% of the urban population live in poor shanty towns or squatter settlements, or they live on the streets. Of Rio de Janeior's 10.6 million resident, for example, 4 million live in squatter settlements and shanty towns, some perched precariously on step hillsides. Nevertheless cities, in developing countries continue to attract more and more people.

Table 3.1: Megacities of the World

Cities with 10 Million or More Inhabitant, 1975, 2000 and 2015 (Population in Million)

City-1975	*Population*	*City-2000*	*Population*	*City-2015*	*Population*
Tokyo	19.8	Tokyo	26.4	Tokyo	26.4
New York	15.9	Mexico City	18.1	Bombay	26.1
Shanghai	11.4	Bombay	18.1	Lagos	23.2
Mexico City	11.2	Sao Paulo	17.8	Dhaka	21.1
Sao Paulo	10.0	Shanghai	17.0	Sao Paulo	20.4
		New York	16.6	Karachi	19.2
		Lagos	13.4	Mexio city	19.2
		Los Angeles	13.1	Shanghai	19.1
		Calcutta	12.9	New York	17.4
		Buenos Aires	12.6	Jakarta	17.3
		Dhaka	12.3	Calcutta	17.3
		Karachi	11.8	Delhi	16.8
		Delhi	11.7	Metro Manila	14.8
		Jakarta	11.0	Low Qngeles	14.1
		Osaka	11.0	Buenos Aires	14.1
		Metro Manila	10.9	Cairo	13.8
		Beijing	10.8	Istanbul	12.5
		Rio de Janeior	10.6	Beijing	12.3
		Cairo	10.6	Rio de Janeior	11.9
				Osaka	11.0
				Tianjin	10.7
				Hyderabad	10.5
				Bangkok	10.1

Source: UN Population Division, March 2000 (p:239).

Cities occupy only 2% of the world's land surface, but city populations have a disproportionate impact on the environment. For example, London requires rough 60 times its land area to supply its 9 million residents with food and forest products. Because commerce and trade have spread dramtically in recent years, city resident consume resources not just from surrounding areas, but, increasingly, from around the world. Urban areas also export their wastes and pollutants, affecting environmental and health conditions far from the cities themselves.

What can be done?

In the long run, slowing population growth would help ease the pressure on cities, buying time to make improvements in technology. Municipalities also can take a number of steps now—building better transportation systems, promoting recycling, and encouraging water conservation.

Public Transportation: One of the best investments that cities can make - both environmental and economic is an efficient mass transportation system. In many cities people waste great amounts of time and fuel going nowhere because traffic congestion is servere. In many urban areas vehicular exhausts account for 50% to 70% of polluting emissions, curbing the number of motor vehicles by offering transportation alternatives would save energy and reduce pollution. Some cities for example, Amsterdam and Copenhagen—have helped ease the transportation crisis by creating special traffic lanes for bicycles and by urging bicycle use.

Recycling: Recycling mountains of urban waste into new resources makes sense both environmentally and economically. Recycling saves natural resources and reduces the amount of trash deposited in landfills or dumped into rivers, lakes, and the ocean. Also, for every million tons of solid waste, about 1,600 recycling jobs could be created in developed and developing countries alike.

Water Conservation: Urbanization dramatically increase per capita freshwater use, as millions of households gain access to piped water, as industry increases, and as large-scale irrigated agriculture replaces subsistence farming. Cities everywhere need to adopt water conservation measures.

Cities Residents to the Rescue 4

In the next ten years, the number of people living in cities will rise to around 3.3 billion. Tokyo already has population of 27 million, Sao Paulo (Brazil) 16.4 million, and Bombay 15 million. World Bank forecasts show as much as 80 per cent of the developing countries economic growth occurring in the cities and major conurbations.

There are both positive and negative aspects to these developments, At each stage in the history of urbanisation, environmental conditions in cities were improved dramatically. The process was often slow, but over time, many epidemic diseases have been controlled, the supply of clean water and the removal of wastes have become routine, the risks of fire have been contained, and standards of comfort and cleanliness have risen to unprecedented levels. Cities could not have become a large and as numerous as they are now if environmental conditions has remained unchanged.

In a curious way, the pollution that cities suffer is largely due to their wealth. The rich consume a great deal more energy, water, building materials and other goods than the poor, and thus produce much more waste. This is what is happening; in the cities where rapid industrialisation is taking place—only the rich enjoy the benefit of piped water and refuse collection.

Increasingly Insanitary Conditions

There is another, often tragic, aspect to this situation. The poorest of the poor are reduced to living in outer-edge shantytowns in extremely insanitary conditions and, lacking the resources to deal with the problem, the city as a whole has to endure congestion and air and water pollution. Some towns and cities are expanding at a rate of over 7 per cent a year, municipal sanitation departments are no longer able to cope, and it is estimated that as many 30 per cent of the population are without running water.

In Many of The World's major runaway population growth, an epidemic of Aids and rising social tensions have been combined in the last few years with a steep drop in incomes. The population living on the outer edges of the cities continues to grow apace, hundreds of thousands of people are without running water and 15 per cent of them without sanitation of any sort. Various volountary bodies and on-governmental organisation have got together, often successfully.

Water and The Environmental Crisis

One key problem concerns the availability of clean water. Some progress has been achieved as a result of the International Drinking Water Supply and Sanitation Decade, but in 1994 at least 220 million people still lacked a source of drinking water near their homes. In some cases, communities of 500 or more inhabitants are served by a single tap. In some towns, communal taps function for only a few hours a day, so that people cannot build up sufficient reserves of water for their personal needs if it takes too long to fetch or if the water has to be carried long distances.

As there are no proper sanitation measures, the disadvantaged members of the population have to drink dirty water, fish in polluted streams, and eat vegetables that have been grown by the side of refuse tips.

A further major problem arises from the threefold harmful impact of cities on the environment; urban development on agricultural land, the extraction and exhaustion of natural resources, and the dumping of refuse.

Growing pressure on coastal regions, where nearly a billion people now live, is doing serious damage to the marine environment. Development activities pose a threat to nearly half the world's coasts.

Towns originally offered people a place of refuge, of mutual help and culture. According to nineteenth-century town-planning theorists, they should supply all human needs. They were supposed to be the very stuff of civilisation. That was not to be, and therefore whenever the authorities throw their hands, dismayed by the scale of the problems and lacking the political will, money or resources to cope with them, personal initiatives are those most likely to succeed.

In Defence of the City Urban Development a Key for Survival

5

The figures sound alarming. The towns and cities in developing countries are growing faster than ever before. By the year 2000, 2.2 billion people will live in the cities of the Third World. Their numbers are expected to double by the year 2025. But many of the cities in Africa, Asia and Latin America are already bursting at the seams. Some of the so-called megacities have more than 10 or 15 million inhabitants. Many of them live in unplanned squatter settlements, without water and electricity, in an environment of squalor, poverty, crime and disease, Nevertheless, the cities seem to have lost nothing of their attraction for the rural populations. Although the larger share of the population increase in the cities of developing countries is caused by the children of people already living there, the rural-urban migration continues unabated. The cities still offer better chances for employment and education, they provide a better physical infrastructure, better health facilities and a more interesting life. Miserable as conditions in the cities often appear to be, they are usually much better than those in the rural areas. It is, therefore, an illusion to believe that the growth of the cities could be checked by concentrating the development efforts on the countryside. There is no alternative to urban development in a world will soon count some 8 billion people.

Cities have always been in the vanguard of development. The ancient civilizations of Mesopotamia, Egypt, Greece and Rome were city cultures which for the first time in human development created large, well-governed states. In Europe during the Middle Ages, the creation of towns and cities offered the rural populations a chance to evade the oppression by feudal authorities and become free citizens. Local self-government in medieval towns is at the cradle of democratic development. There is a clear separation of competence between the national, state and local level of government leaving citizens an opportunity to decide on matters which directly affect their own local environment. It is worth looking at this model when discussing ways organized to improve city governance and allow for more participation of the population.

Another fact worth looking at is the size of cities in Industrialized countries. Although about three-quarters of the people live in urban areas, there are only a handful of really big cities.

Of course, the growth of towns and cities in developed countries is the result of a long historical process, deeply rooted in the particular political and economic conditions of the past centuries. In developing countries today, other conditions prevail which favour the emergence of ever bigger urban conglomerations. However, governments are able, thorough appropriate investment and the location of industries educational facilities, or housing policies to influence the settlement trends in their respective countries in favour of smaller cities.

One point seems certain, though, when considering the pros and cons of city development: the severe environmental problems facing mankind today can only be solved if people live in highly concentrated settlements rather than being spread out evenly over the whole countryside. Environment-friendly mass transport, for instance, is only possible in the cities. Fossil fuel consumption which adds to the pollution of the atmosphere will be lower when people live close to their places of work. Their supply with food, water, electricity and social amenities is cheaper and uses up fewer resources when distances are short. The use of land for housing, transport, and industry is less when buildings grow in height rather than space. Even refuse disposal and wastewater management is easier to organize in a big city than in the countryside.

What is important then is not to question the validity of city development, but to make cities and tows a better place to live in. Good city governance, more involvement of the population in decision-making, more attention paid to environmental hazards caused by congestion and low safety standards are some of the demands that must be met to cope with the problems of the cities. There is no reason to bedevil the city as the most successful form of human settlement. Since the times of Babylon, it has also been a place where many different peoples and cultures meet. A generation from now, half the human population will live in cities. We should see this as a chance for human survival.

Urbanisation and Globalisation 6

How we handle globalisation will determine whether our cities and our civilisation will be divided and violent or user-friendly and peaceful. We cannot get a clear picture of urban life in the 21st century, especially in the poor countries of the South, unless we take into account the phenomenon of globalisation, which has already brought dramatic changes makes their first appearance. So it is there too that the great upheavals of the next century will take place.

Globalisation gives shape to the "Global Village". The "information era" that it ushers in compress is time and we are now living in a world speeded up as never before. World-wide urbanisation is proceeding at a similar rate and its pace in the poor countries of the South seems terrifying. By 2025, two-thirds of humanity will be living in cities and towns, where the best opportunities in life tend to be.

Globalisation also accentuates a "new urban geography" in both North and South. Islands of rich consumers are springing up in cities amid an ocean of deprived people. More and more unemployed people, immigrants, minorities and the homeless, are pushed into cities by pressure from "market economies". As a result, all urban area—not just those in the poor countries of the South—will have to deal with growing internal tensions. In New York, for example, the poorest 20 per cent of the population earns 15 times less than the richest 20 per cent.

Cities have always had their smart neighbourhoods and their dangerous areas. But such social and geographical segregation has changed in pace and scale because of the growth in the urban population, the increase in "illegal" migrant and rising uncertainty.

In fact, we have entered a period of historical transition, where discontinuities prevail over adjustment. Radical changes in the nature of production and jobs and the incredible concentration of capital in the hands of the financial sector and speculators weigh much heavier in our lives these days than state's efforts to adjust and improve the market economy. Segregation in cities has been given a new lease of life whose consequences we do not know. It has reached unprecedented dimensions because of the explosive growth of urban areas.

According to one scenario, things will go badly. The growing pace of globalisation will increase uncertainty about the future. Fear and defence mechanisms will grow among people and institutions, fuelling intolerance, xenophobia and mistrust of everything new or foreign. Urban tensions will manifest themselves with increasing violence, and segregation will sharpen. Public areas will be abandoned and become dangerous no-man's lands, the wretched abode of society's rejects. Cities will lose their original function of being a crossroads for meeting and exchange.

If globalisation also continues to go hand in hand with deregulation of financial markets and an unchanged level of indebtedness of poor countries, the latter will not be able to maintain their urban infrastructures. And if on top of this there is corruption and lack of political will, challenges to system will increase and violence will grow. Cash-strapped authorities will respond with undemocratic mafias which provide them with funds.

According to a second scenario, everything will be all right. In line with the principle that "everything the state does is public, but the state doesn't control everything that is public," a new social contract will be drawn up between the state, the market, the working population and civil society, including NGOs. Cities will develop a new quality of life by providing citizens with forum for exchange. Jobs will be created in the social sector, in the fields of the environment, education, research, culture and leisure, opening up possibilities for young people.

In the countries of the South, long-term development strategies will be drafted and urban planning practised, taking advantage of the opportunities provided by globalisation but without falling into its traps. Town planning will become part of the political process, and the state will work with the private sector, monitored by institution of civil society. Adequate housing will be built with the help of micro credit and controls on the price of building materials. Improved infrastructures will enable marginal areas to become part of the civilized part of the city. Democracy will come up with new ways of governing with the help of networks of involved citizens.

In a transitional scenario, action strategies should fall somewhere between these two extremes. They should include social goals so that in big urban areas a society emerges which is founded on participatory democracy and on "capitalism with a human face" or "market socialism".

But the outlook is less clear than ever. Let us hope the present transition will lead rapidly to a new revival of humanism, whose first signs we are already seeing. This would open up the road to a development which is fair, humane and peaceful.

7 Urbanisation and the Environment

Is abandoning the cities the answer to the growing ecological problems of urbanisation? The trend at any rate is in the opposite direction. At the beginning of this century, only every 10th person worldwide was a city dweller. At its end, more than half the global population will be urbanites. And most of the urban population growth will take place in the developing countries, led by Asia.

Compared to other parts of the world, however, the urbanisation process in Asia is currently not even particularly far out in front. Worldwide, city dwellers account for 43 per cent of the total population. Industrial nations have an average urbanisation rate of 72 per cent. Less industrialized countries have 34 per cent. In the Asia-Pacific region the rate is 30 per cent, in Latin America 72 per cent, and in Africa 33 per cent. The urbanisation growth rate in a number of Asian countries has in fact slowed compared with earlier years. Nevertheless, not only industrialisation, but also the increasing degree of urbanisation has emerged as a growing burden on the environment in many Asian countries.

Changed Urbanisation Pattern in India

Environment burdens are just as much a problem in the old industrial nations as they are in India. But each group has a specific pattern of development. The urbanisation process in India has proven to be more pollution-intensive than that in the old industrial nations of Europe and North America. There are several reasons for that:

- industrialisation in India is restricted to a few locations which are often concentrated in and around capital cities. Although environmental damage continues to be minor at a national level, these locations have higher pollution levels than those ever reached in Industrial nations;

- furthermore, besides the strong regionalisation of industries, the industrialisation pattern of India shows a great diversity of environmental hazards. The trend to establish "last industries first", which is promoted by progressive industrialisation, leads to a country producing certain dangerous materials before they have been covered by state regulations;
- the time factor has to be seen as an important element in the emergence of these already highly regionalized environmental burdens. In India industrialisation and its concomitant urbanisation is taking place within a ban population grew tremendously.

Growing Environmental Damage

Water pollution in India is caused mainly by domestic sewage. For example, households are responsible for 75 per cent of the pollution of the rivers. The domestic sewage problem got more and more out of control with growing urban population. Pipe-based waste water systems are rare in this country. In India dealing with waste has an extremely low priority. The type of waste disposal depends mostly on what the cities can afford. The present level of air pollution is also very high.

Innovative Approaches to Solutions

Environmental protection and economic development are seen as contradictions. Economic development can only be achieved at the cost of higher levels of environmental pollution. And in reverse, if pollution is to be controlled and reduced this can only be done to the disadvantage of further development. In the meantime, however, numerous instances of successful urban environmental management are developing. They could help to change and subsequently break through the existing pattern of thinking. The following approaches can be viewed as important.

Combining regulations with incentives: The introduction of lead-free petrol and the mandatory equipping of new cars with catalytic converters is still by no means common in India. As numerous cars without catalytic converters are still able to use lead-free. Converters were then at first made compulsory for higher-powered cars, and later also for compact models.

Combining regulations with simple controls: Apart from general limitation of the number of cars in the city, its most important single measure to prevent traffic jams and the additional petrol consumption and pollutant emissions caused by them.

High economic growth in India has in fact led to a general reduction of poverty. But the distribution of income, particularly between urban and rural areas, has remained relatively constant. Urban environmental and traffic problems have increased heavily during the same period. These developments can be attributed to a certain pattern of official action (or "non-action"):

- governments have made efforts in supplying roads, but neglected the demand for mobility.
- governments are preoccupied with supplying water, and have neglected follow up problems, above all the questions of waste water disposal and treatment. In Indian cities, for example, this leads to the absurd situation that due to the mushroom like growth of the cities and the increased water pollution linked with it, water must be brought in over ever greater distances and at ever greater expense;
- governments take a one-sided look at noxious substances. Concentrations of harmful substances in water and in the air are in fact checked, and some measures are taken against individual pollutants of single sectors (e.g. lead emissions by the transport sector).

But an integrated policy which operates integrated environmental management with the aim of comprehensively relieving the burdens on the environment has not yet been developed anywhere. To consider such a concept, it is necessary to cut loose from the customary way of approaching problems. It makes sense not to separate the problem areas from each other according to sectors and pollutants, but rather on the basis of their ecological impact.

Orienting on demand hits the core of the concept of ecological modernisation, which is about reducing the intensity of resource use (note, at this stage this does not yet mean the absolute reduction of inputs). At the same time, sights are set on a lower use of land with the same size of population, or also lower energy :onsumption with the same degree of added value or the same per capita income.

Finally, the importance of governments for creating framework conditions must be emphasised once again. Because the actors come from different spheres, such conditions are essential.

From the time of the Greek polis, it was the ambition of the Greek city councillors to pass on a city that was more beautiful than the one they had taken over. There is a long way to go before such an attribute asserts itself in India (and elsewhere).

Urbanisation in India and Limitations 8

Urban growth is an undeniable fact of the future in India. Only 1 in 10 people lived in cities when this century began; nearly half will by century's end. Urban migration accounts for a large share of this rapid growths. Upto 60 per cent of the people in many cities in India live in burgeoning, impoverished squatter settlements.

Allowing urban development to spread out upon undisturbed land exacerbates automobile dependence and destroys the natural environment. Yet it is impossible to truly halt development; prohibiting growth in one jurisdiction merely shifts it to neighbouring areas, The key to a livable and viable future for the India's urban areas is neither to encourage sprawled growth nor to try to stifle growth altogether-but rather, to encourage compact growth.

Forward-looking Municipalities have discovered that compact development can accommodate expanding populations without despoiling the surrounding environment. These cities are actually using urban growth to their advantage: for example, compact development, by making public transit, cycling, and walking more practical, reduces reliance on cars so that less energy is used and less pollution generated. Filling in their under-used space has allowed these cities to become more pleasant and convenient places to live. With less space paved over for parking lots and urban highways, more room is available for homes, workplaces, and green space.

In the long run, population stabilization—via more effective family planning and elimination of poverty—is essential to the future of the Indian cities. But it will take decades to stabilize population growth. In the mean-time it is essential for urban areas to begin redesigning themselves. With compact development, urban areas can meet people's expanding needs by making the most of existing space.

Somewhere to Grow

Many cities have so much underused space that they could develop for decades to come without bulldozoing another square yard of undisturbed land. Although much underuse of property results from individuals and companies holding it for speculation, local governments themselves frequently hold large amounts of vacant real estate. Surplus government buildings, and other public holdings often stay idle while growth mushrooms a the city's edge. In India great potential for filling in underused space lies in redistributing urban land ownership. Land reform, granted, is among the most the most difficult political moves a government can undertake, Yet the need for such an effort is difficult to deny.

Cities have tremendous scope for making urban growth more compact by establishing urban growth boundaries outside of which further development is prohibited. Greenbelts surrounding cities perform this function in India. Cities of strict land-use planning charge that urban growth boundaries and other bold measures encroach on individual freedoms. Yet guiding development more rationally can in fact do more to protect people's rights, while keeping cities livable.

Urban Density: The Real Story

Often, people move out to the suburbs seeking open space and bonds with nature that come only in a rural setting. Yet most of these residents continue to maintain an urban life style—commuting to jobs in the city and demanding an assortment of urban amenities found in suburban shopping malls. The result is neither urban nor rural living, but a destructive compromise that the environment cannot sustain.

The low-density suburban model not only has come at a high ecological price, but it also has failed to deliver on many of its promises. Seeking freedom, mobility, fresh air, and access to open space, many suburbanites instead encounter long commutes and traffic jams caused by the dispersed communities' nearly exclusive reliance on private automobiles. Suburban life promises escape from crime in the city, only to trade that danger for the far greater chance of being injured or killed in a car accident. And a new form of social inequity has emerged, stranding anyone who cannot drive or afford a car.

Although denser land use could help solve the environmental, social, and aesthetic problems of sprawl, widespread misconceptions about increased density—even moderate density—often prevent communities from adopting compact land use strategies. Contrary to popular belief, augmenting the density of development does not create a harsh physical environment. Planners and citizens, often assume that moderate and high-density land use are synonymous with crime, poverty, and squalor. Yet there is no scientific evidence to support a direct link between these social problems and density.

Transport's Missing Link

One of the most destructive by products of low-density sprawl is an automobile-dependent transport system. The pattern of urban development dictates whether people can walk or cycle to work or whether they need to travel dozens of miles; it also determines whether a new bus or rail line can attract enough riders. Despite this obvious link, city layouts often are too dispersed to foster efficient transportation. Many of the India's cities have failed to implement compact land use as a transport strategy; few foresaw that an automobile orientation would later plague them with traffic jams, deadly accidents, harmful noise, and smog, while marginalizing people who do not own cars. A more rational approach for Indian cities would be to integrate homes not only with workplaces but with commercial, recreational, and other land uses so they are easily accessible without cars. Such reforms ideally would not hamper developers or impose uniformity, but instead would lift restriction that create unnaturally one-dimensional districts.

The key to making integrated zoning work well as a transport strategy is to encourage urban development that is dense enough to promote alternatives to cars. For example, transport planners estimate that an Indian city typically requires at least seven dwellings per acre in a given area to support reasonably frequent local bus service, nine dwellings for light rail, and 15 dwellings for an express bus. These moderate densities can be reached by mingling clusters of single-family homes with garden apartments and two-to six-story apartment buildings.

Many large cities are finding that the most transport-efficient land use pattern combines a compact, well-mixed downtown with several outlying, high-density areas—all linked by an extensive public transport system. This way, people can walk, cycle, and take short public transport trips within a given area and reach other areas via express bus or rapid light rail.

Room Enough for All

Attempts to slow or stop growth shut out many groups of people—any by restricting the supply of housing, tend to inflate home prices. Compact growth, by contrast, can help create diverse communities and promote smaller, more affordable housing.

Cities of India can combine compact growth with strategies to increase the supply of land available for low and moderate-income homes. India can made use of measures to prevent speculation, a process whereby land-owners in nearly all free-market societies hold land as an investment for future wind-fall gains, rather than putting it to current use. Speculation puts upward pressure on real estate prices and idles great amounts of urban land.

By taxing vacant land according to its true worth in the market, cities can make these parcels less attractive as an investment vehicle. Local governments typically assess such properties at far less than their market value, effectively rewarding property owners for keeping their land idle. More accurate property assessment encourages redevelopment. Cities can go a step further to tax vacant land more heavily than developed parcels. To avoid spurts of sprawled growth, however, it is critically important to combine these tax strategies with clearly defined growth frontiers—such as greenbelts and urban growth boundaries—that contain development within the existing urban area.

Municipalities can enhance the supply of affordable housing require each house to occupy its own spacious lot with controls that promote a variety of housing types, including smaller and multi-family homes.

A more immediate remedy to the housing crunch felt in many cities, where homes tend to be large, is to allow single-family home owners to rent out small apartments within their homes. The size of the average household is shrinking steadily as couples have fewer children and more people choose living arrangements other than the nuclear family. As a result, many homes built for larger households can create an extra unit in a converted basement, garage, attic, or even an added story.

Laying the Groundwork

Creating compact cities requires a commitment by planning authorities and governments at the local, regional and national levels. Adequate local planning institutions are especially lacking in the developing world. Municipal government in India often have neither the authority to guide land use not the funds to provide basic services. With few exceptions, urban planning is a relatively recent phenomenon in India.

Compact growth of cities also hinges on regional cooperation, an important tool for handling conflicts between the interests of individual localities and those of the broader region. All cities in India are required to plan their own development according to stipulated goals, such as energy conservation, protection of open space, and provision of affordable housing. These statewide planning requirements not only enhance regional cooperation, but they also give cities the backing they need to apply a comprehensive, long-term vision to their land use planning.

Finally, the effectiveness of urban planning can be fully achieved only if governments remove the conflicting incentives posed by other national policies. Among the greatest barriers to compact urban development are artificially low petrol prices, which encourage dependence on cars.

If the barriers to efficient land use were removed, what would a compact city look like? Much of the vast space normally devoted to automobile parking in a sprawled, car-dependent city would be planted in trees and flowers, or used for building homes. Old properties would be received for new uses; a 19th-century warehouse into apartments, a vacant lot into a public park, for instance, the downtown area would be lived in day and night, with apartments and offices occupying the floors above ground-level shops. Each district would be home to a variety of jobs, shops, and day care centres, all within an easy walk or bicycle ride. People could travel quickly to other parts of the city and outlying areas via rapid rail and express bus lines.

On a rapidly urbanizing India, societies can take greater command of their fate by more consciously determining the use of urban land. Whether surrounded by affluent suburbs or makeshift shantytowns, the cities can protect the environment and better address the needs of current and future generations by planning for compact growth.

9 Population Growth and Urbanisation

The world's cities are growing far faster than its population. Indeed, aside from the growth of population itself, urbanisation is the dominant demographic trend of the half-century now ending. In 1950, 750 million of the world's people lived in cities. By 1996, this had at least tripled, to more than 2.6 billion. The number projected to live in cities by 2050, some 6.5 billion people, exceeds world population today.

Urbanisation on anything like the scale that we know today is historically quite recent. In 1800, only one city-London-had a million people. Today, 326 cities have at least that many people. And there are 14 mega cities, those with 10 million or more residents Tokyo is the largest at 27 million. Mexico City is second, at 17 million. New York City and Sao Paulo are close behind, with 16 million each. Rounding out the list in descending size are Bombay (15 million), Shanghai (14), Los Angeles (12) Calcutta (12) Buenos Aires (12), Beijing (11) Osaka (11), Lagos (10), Rio de Janeiro (10), and Delhi (10).

The rate of growth of cities in industrial countries during the first century or so of the Industrial Revolution was relatively slow; Today's cities are growing much faster. It took London 130 years to get from 1 million to 8 million. Mexico City made this jumps in just 30 years.

Measured in annual growth, some cities, such as Lagos, Nigeria, are growing at 5 per cent a year; Bombay is growing at nearly 4 per cent. The world's urban population as a whole is growing by just over 1 million people each week. This urban growth is fed by natural increase of urban populations, by net migration from the countryside, and by villages, by net migration from the countryside, and by villages or towns expanding to the point where they become cities or they are absorbed by the spread of existing cities.

During the early stages of industrialisation, urbanisation was largely in response to the pull of employment opportunities in cities. More recently, however, the movement from countryside to city has been more the result of rural push than of urban pull. It is a reflection of the lack of opportunity in the countryside as already small plots of land are divided and then divided again with each passing generation, until they become so small that people can no longer make a living from them.

Historically, cities and the surrounding countryside had a symbolic relationship, with the latter supplying food and raw materials in exchange for manufactured products. Today cities are tied much more to each other and to the global economy. The food and fuel that once came from the surrounding countryside now often comes from distant corners of the planet.

As societies urbanize, the use of basic resources, such as energy, and water, rises. In traditional rural societies, for example, people live on the land and thus do not need to travel to work. But once they migrate to cities, commuting becomes the rule, not the exception. In villages, most of the food that is consumed is produced locally, requiring little energy for processing, packaging, and transportation; once people move into cities, on the other hand, virtually all their food must be brought in. In a village where residents typically draw their water from a central well and carry it to their homes, water use in necessarily limited. But when villagers move to urban high-rise apartment buildings with indoor plumbing, replete with shower and flush toilets, water consumption soars.

The ecology of cities is a continuing challenge to city managers simply because cities require the concentration of huge quantities of water, food, energy and raw materials. The waste products must then be dispersed or he city will become uninhabitable. As cities become larger, the disposal of residential and industrial wastes becomes ever more challenging.

Partly as a result of the mounting pressure for people to migrate to cities, the growth in urban populations is far outstripping the availability of basic services, such as water, sewerage, transportation, and electricity. As a result, life in urban shantytowns is plagued by poverty, pollution, congestion, homelessness, and unemployment.

Since the beginning of the Industrial Revolution, the terms of trade between countryside and city have favoured the latter simply because cities control the scarce resources in development, namely capital and technology. But if the price of food rises in the years ahead, as now seems likely, the terms of trade could shift, favouring the countryside. If in the new world of the twenty-first century the scarce resources are land and water, those controlling them could have the upper hand in determining rural/urban terms of trade.

This aside, if recent trends continue, within the next several years more than half of us will be living in cities-making the world more urban than rural for the first time in history. We will have become an urban species, far removed from our hunter-gatherer origins.

Stop Child Labour 10

Although the internationally recommended minimum age for work 10 is far from negligible, almost all the data available on child labour concerns the is 15 years and the number of child workers under the age of 10-to-14 age group.

Traditionally, the proportion of working children has been much higher in rural than in urban areas—nine out of ten are engaged in agricultural or related activities. In the towns and cities of India where child labour has increased steadily as a result of the rapid urbanization of recent years, working children are found mainly in trade and services and to a lesser extent in the manufacturing section.

Available statistics suggest that more boys than girls work. It should be borne in mind, however, that the number of working girls is often under estimated by statistical surveys, as they usually do not take into account full-time housework performed by many children, the vast majority of whom are girls, in order to enable their parents to go to work.

Girls, moreover, tend to work longer hours, on average, than do boys. This is especially true for the many girls employed a domestic workers, a type of employment in which hours of work are typically extremely long. This is also the case of girls employed in other types of jobs who, in addition to their professional activity, must help with the housework in their parents' home.

One of the factors affecting the supply of child labour is the high cost, in real terms, of obtaining an education. Many children work to cover the costs of school expenses. But, many schools serving the poor are of such abysmal equality or chances of upward mobility for graduates are so slim, that the expected return is not equal to the sacrifice made... While it is true that many children drop out of school because they have to work, it is equally true that many become so discouraged by school that they prefer to work.

In manufacturing industries, children are most likely to be employed when their labour is less expensive or less troublesome than that of adults, when other labour is scarce, and when they are considered irreplaceable by reason of their size or perceived dexterity.

Many working children face significant threats to their health and safety. The majority are involved in farming and are routinely exposed to harsh climate, sharpened tools, heavy loads as well, increasingly, as a to toxic chemicals and motorized equipment. Others, particularly girls working as domestic servants away from their homes, are frequent victims of physical, mental and sexual abuses which can have devastating consequences on their health.

Prostitution is another type of activity in which children, especially girls, are increasingly found. The AIDS epidemic is a contributing factor to this trend, as adults see the use of children for sexual purposes as the best means of preventing infection. The laissez-faire attitude of the authorities incharge of national and international tourism is also largely responsible for the current situation.

Another extremely serious problem is child slavery in India. A large number of child slaves are to be found in agriculture domestic, help, the sex industry, the carpet and textile industries, quarrying and brickmaking." Child slavery predominates mainly where there are social systems based on the exploitation of poverty, such as debt bondage, when the motivation is the debt incurred by a family to meet a social of religious obligation or simply to acquire the means of survival.

There is a growing body of opinion that national and international efforts need to be more sharply focussed on the most abusive and hazardous forms of child labour, granting them first concern and priority. Perhaps the most telling social argument against child labour is that its effects are highly discriminatory, adding to the burden and disadvantage of individuals and groups already among the socially excluded while benefiting those who are privileged. For that reason, child labour is inconsistent with democracy and social justice.

Action Required at the National Level

In the majority of states of India where child labour is common, the action taken until now to combat it has in no way been proportional to the extent and gravity of the problem. Many state governments have left it to economic growth and legislation alone to provide the solution. Experience has shown however that, unless specific measures are taken, growth in itself rarely benefits the very poor and that legislation means little where it is not vigorously enforced.

The problem of child labour will not be solved overnight. It is one of the many facets of poverty and underdevelopment. Resources available to reduce its extent and damaging effects are by definition scarcest in India that need them the most. Priorities must therefore be set.

No Effective Programmes Without Hard Information

Research: Almost everywhere, hard information is lacking on how many children are working, what they are doing, where and in what conditions. Without such data, it is virtually impossible to develop effective policies and porgrammes. Establishing, in some cases improving, data collection systems on child labour is an essential first step.

Raising Awareness: A common attitude toward child labour in India is to accept it as an unavoidable consequence of poverty. Given the low quality and implied costs of the education services available to the poor, many parents, having themselves worked as children, tend to consider an early entry into the labour markets, rather than schooling, as the best way to equip their children with skills useful for their future as adults.

Another difficulty is inherent in the fact that children working in rural areas, in urban informal sector workshops or as domestic servants in private households are not readily visible. An effective effort to protect children from work place hazards or abuses must therefore begin by making the invisible visible. Experience clearly shows that significant public pressure is required to make progress on the child labour issue politically possible. As long as the general public, and in particular the middle and higher classes, consider that child labour is part of the harsh reality that makes good economic sense, the conditions for change will not be met.

The Government of India has restricted its role to enacting legislation, but has been passive in its enforcement. Most initiatives against child labour have traditionally come from Non-Government Organisations. In spite of their dedication however, their resources cannot be equal to the magnitude of the task. All levels of society need to do their share.

Some types of action can be provided only by the central government: child labour legislation and attendant enforcement mechanisms, the setting of public policy priorities and a publicly-funded system of basic education that offers quality schooling for all, including the children of the poorest families.

Trade Unions Bring Abuses to Light

Trade unions, are the logical leaders for bringing child labour abuses to light. They are ideally placed to document concrete cases of abusive child labour and to monitor the effectiveness of legal instruments and the performance of the labour inspectorate in the child labour field.

Employers and their organisations also have good reasons to be interested in the issue. Besides obvious humanitarian and social reasons, combating child labour makes perfect sense on economic and business grounds. Emotionally or physically damage children have little chance of becoming productive adults.

NGOs' Strength is with Children Already Working

Like trade unions, NGOs can help to discover and publicize specific cases of abusive child labour. They are, in addition especially good at devising and implementing action programmes on behalf of children already in the labour market. Close to the children, the generally enjoy that trust of the local communities concerned and are well placed to appeal to their hearts and resources.

The participation of other segments of civil society—the media, universities, parliamentarians, teachers and educators—should be enlisted in the fight against child labour. All are valuable allies and can cooperate in complementary ways.

Establishing the required institutional capacity: To formulate and execute a national plan of action against child labour, institutional mechanisms must be established or strengthened within the governmental apparatus. These can then be entrusted with the responsibility for setting priorities, coordinating the activities of the various ministries concerned, promoting private sector participation and for launching and supporting pilot schemes to find new ways of preventing child labour and of rehabilitating those who have been rescued from it.

Improving legislation and enforcement measures: In India legislation expemts from coverage precisely the kinds of work in which children are most engaged (agriculture, family undertakings, small workshops, domestic service). A necessary first step to expanding protection under the law is to ensure that the main places where children work and the worst forms of child labour are encompassed by national legislation.

Improving schooling for the poor: The single most effective way to stem the flow of school-age children into abusive forms of employment or work is to extend and improve schooling so that it will attract and retain them. Recent trends however leave little room for optimism in that regard. In the eighties and early nineties resources devoted to education have dwindled steadily in India. The poor situation of the economy and the effects of structural adjustment policies were the reasons generally given for this decline.

Using economic incentives: As poor families need the income deriving from the employment of their children, it has often been considered appropriate to provide cash or in-kind payments as replacement.

Lively international debate over negative incentives: The advisability of using negative economic incentives has been the subject of much recent public debate. In Europe several department stores have decided not to sell products such as carpets unless they are certified to be made without child labour. Such movements by consumers and manufacturers alike have been accompanied by powerful efforts on the legislative and trade fronts as demonstrated by the hot debate on the incorporation of a social clause into international trade agreements. The United States has introduced conditionality into its Generalized System of Preferences, as has the European Union, to promote, among others, better labour standards and thereby discourage the use of child labour. A bill aiming at banning the import into the United States of Goods produced by children (the Harkin Bill), has generated concern among employers and governments in countries heavily dependent on the United States for their exports.

There is no doubt that initiatives of this kind have helped significantly to raise public awareness about child labour. However, they have also had unintended consequences. The mere threat led employers of various industries to abruptly dismiss tens of thousands of children, the end result was that.

11 Child Labour in Weaving Industry

Approximately 1,30,000 children work in India's hand-knotted carpet industry. The working conditions are often poor, involving long hours sitting in one position, breathing cotton and wool fibres, eye-strain from doing very fine work and poor lighting. In the smallest enterprises the only light often available is the natural light filtering in through an open doorway.

Children are more likely to work in larger establishments: the smallest enterprises are family operations where the father and other family members might both weave carpets and till a plot of land, whereas the larger buisness use almost all hired labour, In the one-loom enterprises, approximately 14% of weavers are children, while the number of a child labourers rises to around 33% in businesses with five or more looms.

Although the proportion of child labour rises with the size of firm, the proportion doesnot rise as the quality of carpet increases; in fact, children are more likely to work on low-quality than on the highest-quality carpets. Ther is "no evidence that children dominate any particular design or quality niches". The opposite would be the case if the "nimble flingers" argument were true.

If the "nimble fingers" argument does not hold in the hand-knotted carpet industry, then it probably doesnot hold in other industries. Rejection of the "nimble fingers" argument is reinforced by the ability of adults to master carpet-weaving skills. Many adolescents and young adults who attend government training centres go on to run their own weaving businesses, while weavers say it takes a year to become fully proficient, whether one starts as an adult or a child.

Enterprises Often Small and Impoverished

The workforce of the hand-knotted carpet industry is mired in poverty. Most weaving enterprises in the Indian hand-knotted carpet industry are small, marginal operations run by poor and illiterate men, and they have no margin to pay higher wages. Most of the employers have never attended school; then began weaving before age 14. An enterprises normally consists of a loom set up in a family's one-room cottage, with perhaps an additional loom, or looms, in an attached verandah or a shed. Male family members, including children, provide the bulk of the labour.

India's Factories Act has influenced the current structure of the carpet industry. Costly health, safety and labour regulations to which large firms are subject do not apply to cottage industries. Only a small proportion of establishment has five or more looms.

Competition Limits Retail Price Increases

While child and adult weavers have similar productivity, there is a cost advantage to hiring child labour: children earn less while apprentices than do fully-trained weavers, and their addition to the workforce depresses the going wage rate. Replacing the 22% of children in the workforce would likely cause the wage bill to rise by about 5%.

Given the small scale of many weaving enterprises and the fact that weaving charges make up approximately 40% of the total production cost, with the loom owner receiving a fee equivalent to 10% of production costs for supervision and provision of looms and premises, it is clear that the use of child labour can add greatly to the revenues and profits of loom owners.

The extra labour costs involved in eliminating child labour become much easier to absorb further down the distribution chain. Importing country wholesalers mark up the carpets around 65% while foreign retailers typically mark up the carpets by approximately 200%. With sales or value-added tax, the carpets can easily cost four times as much to the consumer as the Indian export price. This means that the overall savings in production costs form the use of child labour are very small when compared to the foreign retail price.

Finding solutions which satisfy both local weavers and foreign retailers must avoid a beggar-thy–neighbour spiral. If carpet producing countries simultaneously implemented a no-child-labour strategy in their hand-knotted carpet industries, none of them would be at a competitive disadvantage.

Methods of reducing child labour such as those used in the garment industry where there is tripartite collaboration to ensure that the children are treated well and that there are educational opportunities for them until they are replaced without economic hardship to their families, is not likely to work in the hand-knotted carpet industry. Neither labeling nor inspection is likely to work here because the industry is too fragmented. It is impossible to control the thousands of cottages where one or two carpets per year are woven. We need solutions that address the general problems of poverty while developing alternative source of both employment and education.

Child labour is not necessary in the carpet industry. Children do not possess a unique skill and there is a ready pool of surplus adult labour ready to take over from them. "people should not be fooled into thinking that child labour is necessary for the industry to survive. The irreplaceable skills or "nimble fingers" argument should no longer be used to justify the use of child labour in the carpet industry or any other industry."

Child Labour: *Targeting the Intolerable* 12

We all know that child labour is one of the faces of poverty and that many efforts over many years will be required to eliminate it completely. But, there are some forms of child labour today which are intolerable by any standard. These deserve to be identified, exposed and eradicated without further delay.

The problem of child labour is so enormous and the need for action is urgent, choices must be made about where to concentrate available human and material resources. The most humane strategy must therefore be to focus scarce resources first on the most intolerable forms of child labour such as slavery, debt bondage child prostitution, work in hazardous occupations and industries, and the very young, especially girls.

In addition, a comparative study carried out over a period of 17 years in India on both children who attend school and children who instead work in agriculture, industry or the service sector showed that working children grow up shorter and weigh less than school children.

In Bombay, that health of children working in hotels, restaurants, construction and elsewhere was found to be considerably inferior to that of a control group of non working school children. Working children exhibited symptoms of constant muscular, chest and abdominal pain, headaches, dizziness, respiratory infections, diarrhoea and worm infection.

Sexual Differences

Girls more often work in domestic labour, boys work in construction, fields and factories, leading to sexual differences in exposure to hazards. Girls, because of their employment in households, work longer hours than boys each day. This is one important reason why girls receive less schooling than boys. Girls are also more vulnerable than boys to sexual abuse and its consequences, such as social rejection, psychological trauma and unwanted motherhood. Boys, on the other hand, tend to suffer more injuries resulting from carrying weights too heavy for their age and stage of physical development. There are unsafe and abusive working situations for children. Some examples of these included:

Slavery and Forced Child Labour

Of all working children, those bound in slavery and forced child labour are the most imperiled. Children are still being sold outright for a sum of money. At other times, landlords buy child workers from their tenants, or labour "contractors" pay rural families in advance in order to take their children away to work in carpet-weaving, glass manufacturing or prostitution.

Prostitution and Trafficking of Children

The commercial sexual exploitation of children is on the rise, even though the subject has in recent years become as issue of global concern. Children are increasingly being bought and sold across national borders by organised networks.

Agriculture: Children work in agriculture throughout the world and often face hazards through exposure to biological and chemical agents. Children can be found mixing, loading and applying pesticides, fertilizers or herbicides, some of which are highly toxic and potentially carcinogenic. Pesticide exposure poses a considerably higher risk to children than to adults, and has been linked to an increased risk of cancer, neuropathy, neuro-behavioural effects and immune system abnormalities.

Mortality among child farm workers from pesticide poisoning is greater than from a combination of childhood diseases such as malaria, tetanus, diphtheria, polio and whooping cough. The operation of farm machinery by children also leads to many accidents which kill and maim.

Mining: Child labour is used in small-scale mines in many countries. Child miners work long hours without adequate protective equipment, clothing or training. They are also exposed to high humidity levels and extreme temperatures.

Mining hazards include exposure to harmful dusts, gasses and fumes that cause respiratory diseases that can develop into silicosis, pulmonary fibrosis, asbestosis and emphysema after some years of exposure. Child miners also suffer from physical strain, fatigue and musculoskeletal disorders, as well as serious injuries from falling objects. Children working in gold mines are endangered by mercury poisoning.

Ceramics and glass factory work: Child labour in these industries is common. Children often must carry molten loads of glass dragged from tank furnaces at a temperature of 1500-1800 degrees Centigrade. They also work long hours in rooms with poor lighting and little or no ventilation. The temperature inside these factories, some of which operate only at night, ranges from 40 to 45 degrees Centigrade. Floors are covered with broken glass and in many cases electric wires are exposed. The noise level from glass-pressing machines can be as high as 100 decibels or more, causing hearing impairment.

The main hazards in this industry are exposure to high temperatures leading to heat stress, cataracts, burns and lacerations; injuries from broken glass and flying glass particles; hearing impairment from noise; eye injuries and eye strain from poor lighting; and exposure to silica dust, lead and toxic fumes such as carbon monoxide and sulphur dioxide.

Matches and fireworks industry: Match production normally takes place in small cottage units or in small-scale village factories where the risk of fire and explosion is present at all times. Children as young as three are reported to work in match factories in unventilated rooms where they are exposed to dust, fumes, vapours and airborne concentrations of hazardous substances—asbestos, potassium chlorate, antimony trisulphide, amorphous red phosphorous mixed with sand or powdered glass and tetraphosphorous trisulphide. Intoxication and dermatitis from these substance are frequent.

Deep-sea fishing: In many Asian countries, children work in muro-ami fishing, which involves deep-sea diving without the use of protective equipment. The children beat on coral reefs to scare the fish into nets. Each fishing ship employs up to 300 boys between ages 10 and 15 recruited from poor neighbourhoods. Divers rest the nets several times a day, so that the children are often in the water for up to 12 hours. Dozens of children are killed or injured each year from drowning or from decompression sickness or fatal accidents from exposure to high atmospheric pressure. Predatory fish such as sharks, barracudas, needle-fish and poisonous sea snakes also attack the children.

Child domestic workers: Children domestic service is a widespread practice in many developing countries, with employers in cities often recruiting children from rural villages through family, friends and contacts. Violence and sexual abuse are among the most serious and frightening hazards facing children at work, specially those in domestic service. Such abuse leads to permanent psychological and emotional damage.

Construction: Children undertaking heavy work, carrying massive loads and maintaining awkward body positions for a long time can develop deformation of the spinal column. Sometimes the pelvis can also be deformed because of excessive stress being placed on the bones before the epiphysis has fused. Children working in construction and other fields are exposed to other toxic and carcinogenic substances, including absebstos, one of the best known of human carcinogens.

One reason why modern societies and governments have not been more active in curbing the most harmful forms of child labour is that working children are often not readily visible. It is a matter of 'out of sight' out of mind'.

Helping Your Child Learn 13

A one-syllable word begins the education process: "Why?" Parents are always trying to answer that question. And that interaction between parent and child is the basis of much that children learn.

Teaching and learning are not mysteries that can happen only in school. They can also happen when parents and children do simple things together—things such as:

- Figure out whose socks are whose-sorting is a major function in maths and science.
- Cook a meal to learn science and good health.
- Tell each other a story as an important beginning for reading and writing; if the story is about the past, it's a way to interest a child in history.
- Plan a visit to a friend or relative for a personal connection with geography.
- Or play a game of hopscotch to develop counting and lifelong fitness.
- All children love their friends. So ask your child to describe his friend's appearance at the end of each school day. You can ask questions like. "What outfit did he/she wear?" or "How did he/she do his/her hair? This kind of routine query would encourage your child to observe his friend more minutely.
- If your child goes to school by bus, he can be asked to describe his route and point out certain landmarks namely colourful posters, traffic signals, large shops etc.

By doing things with their children, parents show that learning is fun and important—and that encourages children to study, learn, and stay in school.

Even on the discipline front, parents can help their children. Basic disciplinary principles must be tailored to each child and family. Before parents can become effective disciplinarians, they must first learn how to manage their own anger, solve problem situations and give and get support from others. Simple self-help techniques with or without professional support can help parents sharply reduce discipline problems.

Parents who are sensitive to their children's needs have more obedient children. Praise and love alone are not enough to instil good behaviour. Too much permissiveness hurts a child's efforts to develop self-control.

Behaviour problems should be reversed early. Waiting until the preteen-age years diminishes chances for success and puts children at higher risk for drug use and other problems.

Parents need to learn as many tricks of the trade as possible, including how to play with their children, Communicate with them, praise and reward them and also set limits for them, as well as how to handle misbehaviour using a variety of techniques.

All that parents need to help their children is a willingness to observe and learn with them, and, to take the time to nurture their natural curiosity.

Solving the Unemployment Problem by Looking Beyond the Job 14

If you had a job, you worked; if you didn't, you didn't. Having a job meant being employed by an organisation in a clearly defined and stable occupational role, with duties, hours, rates of pay and promotion all more or less standardized. But the job—in that meaning of the world—is a social invention, and a fairly recent one.

The job—the kind that you had, or hoped to get—became a central fixture of life. Its importance was great because it served many needs: For managers and efficiency experts, job assignments were the key to assembly-line manufacturing. For union organizers, jobs protected the rights of workers. For political reformers, standardized civil service positions were the essence of good government. Jobs provided an identity to immigrants and recently, urbanized farm workers. They provided a sense of security for individuals and an organizing principle for society.

Jobs functioned in so many ways that it is surprising how many organisations are now opting for other ways to define and manage work. The second job shift is underway. Its emergence can be seen in the increasing use of temporary and part-time workers and contracted-out services, the changing relationships between workers and management, the growing popularity of self-employment and small business. Indeed, "de-jobbing" is proceeding at such a pace that many economists, management experts and futurists are now talking freely about the end of the job. Bridges predicts that the job as we now know it will disappear entirely—replaced by new kinds of flexible work assignments in post-job organisations—and be remembered only as a quaint artifact of the industrial age.

One reason for the change in work is the economic rules of the survival game among organisations that employ workers. To stay successful in today's hitech consumer economy, businesses have had to re-model themselves into what some experts call "agile companies"—ones that are able to respond quickly to conditions in ever-changing fragmenting, competitive markets.

The "knowledge worker", whose work involves not simply doing something, but also applying theoretical or analytical skills. Such workers are replacing the industrial labourer as the dominant part of the workforce—and their productive activities are likely to be organized and structured much differently from those of their assembly-line predecessors.

De-jobbing as a result of new technology or the emergence of a service economy is a phenomenon that gets a lot of attention these days; but it is not the whole story. At all levels of society, people are improvising livelihoods that do not fit the industrial-era model. Immigrants to the developed countries, often unable to find steady jobs, nevertheless find places in the new landscape by being mobile, flexible, resourceful and imaginative; they moonlight, work part-time, share jobs, start small businesses. Their lives are often extremely difficult, but they are also instructive to those of us believe you either have a job or you're out of luck.

It is too early to evaluate the implications of this multifaceted transformation of work, or to dismiss it as simply good or bad. Nevertheless, one cannot deny that it is taking place, and will bring about dramatic social changes.

On the downside, the job shift is causing great hardships for many workers and their families. It poses serious challenges to policy-makers, political activists and labour leaders. The basic question appears to be whether the key to global employment-development strategy is to play "catch-up"—trying to bring millions of people around the world into jobs in industries and the public sectors; or to play "leapfrog"—creating new forms of employment.

The proposal to generate more employment in agriculture, for example, is based on new demand for agricultural exports from developing countries. The policies designed to make the most of this opportunity include measures to upgrade technology, raise productivity, ensure the supply of éssential inputs, establish marketing and distribution channels, create links between agriculture and industry, and cater to export markets.

The issue of part-time work, another kind of employment that is seriously undervalued in the traditional industrial—era job mind-set. Part-time work may not offer much at this point to developing countries, where many people are under employed and wages are low, but it can be of great help in more advanced economies. And it is likely to be a big part of the global work picture in the years ahead.

A certain agility may also be necessary in agriculture, particularly in countries that for many years have depended heavily on producing commodities such as sugar for export as a means of generating income and employment. As Northern laborations develop non-agricultural substitutes for many of these commodities—and this is already beginning to happen—the bottom may fall out of "monoculture" economies, only economic, but will have long-run political implications as communities attempt to reorganize themselves in response to the changed conditions. It is, therefore, in the interest of raw materials exporters to closely monitor current trends in biotechnology and the use of genetic resources and modify their internal policies in anticipation of potential long-term effects."

This calls for flexibility, and an ability to get information and to act on it. Government officials, development workers, community leaders and individuals will, in some respects, all have to be "knowledge workers" if they are to keep ahead of global changes. Jobs are going to be created not just by putting people to work, but by finding-or creating-new niches where they can be productive.

It is still possible to talk about jobs for all, and to resist the assumption made by many economists that high levels of unemployment are now inevitable. But, as we move ahead into the global information economy, we may be moving back into an older conception of the job, and seeing it again as something you do, rather than as something you have—or that has you.

15 Democracy and the Market Economy

Today the idea of democracy is triumphant; the model is in principle embraced in most countries the world over. You may say that the very word democracy has been hailed and misused earlier in history. The most repressing and totalitarian regimes have tried to mask themselves as "real" or "peoples" democracies. What has happened, however, is a historical demasking of these false pretences.

What exactly do we mean by democracy? There is now a general agreement that democracy cannot be defined by purpose or policy or levels of mass mobilisation. It must be defined as a political system where different parties or individuals compete for power through regular free elections where all adult citizens have a vote. Moreover, a democracy must uphold certain basic human rights and well-defined freedoms which make the political process possible, and respect the opinion and integrity of the individual. No other definitions hold, and we should be careful when we talk about "real" democracy versus "formal" democracy. A society, which in real life upholds the constitutional or formal democratic principles and which in practice applies the rights these principles imply, is by definition a democracy. A society with a beautiful-sounding constitution but where none or few of these rights are respected is certainly not a democracy.

Democratic Government No Guarantee for Equality

It is important to understand that democratic government does not necessarily mean good government in the sense that those in power make wise or well-considered decisions. Nor does it mean that conflicts inherent in the society are reduced to a minimum. Demands for democracy, social justice and a better life have historically gone hand in hand, but this does not mean that the establishment of a democratic system actually does lead to an improvement in social conditions or equality. It is also quite clear that some societies have a sort of outer shell of democracy but in reality, exclude large groups of people from having any political influence whatsoever. The actual differences in living conditions are so enormous and so entrenched that these people have no confidence at all in the political system even if it is democratic according to the definition. In these cases—for example in some Latin American countries—one can talk of a "masked hegemony with competing elites" where the outcome of struggles for power has little relevance for the masses. It is a sort of social and political half-authoritarian system-but disguised as a democracy—where the military often have a significant influence.

In the rhetoric of the day the term market economy and democracy are used as if they were synonymous or at least naturally emerging at the same time. But this is wrong—or at least misleading. When the market economy or capitalism finally established itself in the 1800s and came to characterize modern industrial civilisation, democracy was at best in its infancy. In fact one could argue that democracy grew out of the contradictions and social dynamism inherent in the market economy of the capitalistic system. In this century we have a long list of terrifying and repressive regimes, which have nevertheless upheld the virtues of a market economy. That some of these regimes have for ideological and security reason been hailed as bastions against communism, and also dignified members of the so-called free world does not transform them into democracies. In this company it is perhaps unnecessary to remind ourselves that the colonial system was assuredly not democratic, but was certainly based on capitalistic or market economic principles. It is the sad but irrefutable historical coupling between Western democracy, colonialism, and the plundering of resources in the name of the market economy which for understandable reasons meant that many of the leaders of national liberation movements looked for other models for the development of their young nations. In this connection it can be worth remembering what Nelson Mandela said soon after his release from 26 years of prison in the market economic but racist state of South Africa. "When we in ANC during 40 years struggle for democracy we were put in prison by the same people who are now telling us how we should behave to promote the democracy we have been rejected by all these year".

While we can see that a market economy does not automatically lead to democracy, a functioning democracy—as we have defined it-does seem to require some form of free economic system.

Democracy and Economic Freedom

Theoretically, it is conceivable that a political democracy could be combined with an economy totally controlled by the government—but experience has shown this to be very difficult. One could even argue that it is by definition impossible since democracy implies a certain freedom of economic choice and independent economic actors. A functioning democratic system presupposes what is now often referred to as a civil society—in practice, independent institutions, companies, organisations, the media etc., regulated by law but not subject to or controlled by those in power.

We must also see clearly that there are no unambiguous relations between economic growth, development and democracy. Democratic governments are neither very successful when it comes to structural reforms which may be to the disadvantage of important interest in the society, nor when it comes to welfare. The developing countries which have achieved the greatest success economically and socially over the last 20 years are the East Asian countries—which all have had various kinds of more or less authoritarian systems.

However, that does not mean that you can use these countries as models for the rest of the world. There is no globally valid link between an authoritarian form of regime and economic development, not even when development is defined only in terms of autocentric growth. Many social scientist—have tried to find some systematic connection between what we call development or modernisation on the one hand, and the political system on the other—but all have failed.

It is also obvious that one of several pre-requisites for economic growth and development is legitimate and reasonably well functioning government and governance. If the free market is to be a motor for development and improved welfare, and not just a meeting place for robber barons, the mafia and speculators, you must have a regulating and supportive state. If economic history teaches us anything, it is just this. Consider the astounding development in Germany after the war, or in Japan and the other East Asian countries some years later. There are many differences, but what they have in common is a well-functioning government apparatus with a long tradition.

Today we find ourselves in a historical situation where a large number of countries in the former communist states of Europe, in Africa, Asia and Latin America are at one and the same time trying to establish a new democratic system and new economic mechanisms. The situation is unique, and the intrinsic problems are unprecedented. Democracy as an idea has triumphed but in its practice it is in profound trouble. It is no exaggeration to talk of the crisis of democracy.

The former communist countries are certainly in crisis. As by-product of the past regimes, there is an intensive suspicion of the political institutions, of the state and the parties—and in this way also the legitimacy of democracy and the ability of the politicians to deal with the fundamental problems of society has been undermined. The lack of a democratic tradition is not overcome from one day to the next.

Many of the developing countries have similar difficulties. The introduction of a multiparty system does not in itself mean that one can manage the conflicts and social problems in a democratic way.

Countries in Transition

Both in the East and the South countries are trying, at one and the same time, to change the political and economic system. When the whole society is convulsed by economic changes, and where peoples' living conditions fundamentally change, it is easy to develop and maintain a political system based on compromise and respect, including respect for minorities.

As in previous history the deep crises of legitimacy and general frustration feed national and ethnical conflicts. These conflicts establish themselves in societies where the authoritarian system, economic crises and the break down of traditional values rob people of any kind of kinship other than ethnical.

We cannot avoid seeing disturbing signs of this crisis of democracy also in the so-called "established democracies" of the rich countries.

It is obvious that the state of democracy varies from country to country as do the reasons for a feeling of dejection. But there are some similarities too.

The continuing and noticeable internationalisation limits the national freedom of political choice, available alternatives, and makes it more difficult for people to see the connection between "politics" and their actual living conditions. The governments are restrained by international economic events. The reaction of the stock exchange may be more important than that of the voters. The election results influence the stock exchange prices—but is it perhaps not also so that the stock exchange, indirectly, also influence the election results? People feel themselves to be the victims of major economic changes, but no one seems to be responsible and they themselves feel they have little chance of influencing the outcome. The absence of clearly identifiable alternatives between the larger political parties provides between the larger political parties provides opportunities for the populists and the extremists.

There is indeed reason to reflect on the lessons of the history of our turbulent and cruel century.

Priority for Growth

There is today much concern about the lack of resources for such urgent needs as the reconstruction of the East, a concerted attack on poverty and human development in the poorest countries, and environmental investments of all kinds. If the growth of world output returns to the levels of the 1980s, total output would grow by about one trillion dollar a year. There is, infact, no other way to resolve the economic and political crises multiplying in the world community than to give priority to the restoration of growth.

We are certainly not at the end of history as someone has argued. We are rather at a dramatic turning point, a moment of many possibilities and many dangers. What we do now, for a few years ahead, may direct the future for several decades—like the dramatic and fateful years immediately after the second world war. All nations, all governments, have a responsibility. The rich world has a special responsibility, not just moral because of its enormous economic and political power.

Employment and Poverty Alleviation 16

Today the key socio-economic problem is large-scale unemployment. Spreading joblessness brings many other problems in its wake. It erodes national incomes and living standards, aggravating the already grindingly difficult job of promoting development and alleviating poverty. Joblessness also raises government budget deficits, increasing macro-economic instability while soaking up investment for productive capital expenditure, education, training and relief aid. And joblessness ruins lives and communities by depriving people of the dignity and satisfaction that comes with earning one's keep and making a contribution to the well being of family and society.

Theories about how best to nurture development (and thus create jobs) have shifted considerably over the last decade. The state role has evolved, in the minds of many, from being a source of relief for the problems of unemployment, poverty and underdevelopment, to being a fundamental cause of these problems through the distorting impact of its intervention on the market.

However, the more market oriented philosophy that grew up during the 1990s has yet to provide convincing solutions in practice at least not on a grand scale and especially not in terms of job creation as the present jobless economic recovery demonstrates.

The weakness of the current recovery and past approaches to economic development can be traced to the failure to consider employment as the predominant means of promoting growth and alleviating poverty. In policy circles it has too long been an almost ignored priority.

Current trends thus bode poorly, particularly as unemployment rates soar In light of the circumstances, we need to begin re-examining some of the fundamental questions if only to find out what has gone wrong with the answers.

Minimum Wage

Let's begin with wages. With corporate restructuring in full force on a global scale, are low wage rates required to raise employment and maximize profits? A top manager of a multinational consumer electronics group certainly thinks so; he likened the perfect factory to a ship "so that we could move it around the world to where labour was cheapest". Perhaps, but this bottom-line emphasis on unit labour costs ignores at least two other factors; namely, that higher wages can act as a screen to select more productive workers and that higher wages translate into better productivity via improved worker nutrition, increased consumption and a generally healthier quality of life.

If higher wages bring these benefits (and it is an open question) should government insist that there be a minimum wage rate? Neo-classical economists tend to respond "no", assuming that a higher wage rate puts money into the pockets of some low wage workers while forcing many others out of work because companies cannot afford to pay them.

Technology Transfer

The impact of technology is another area in need of study. Technological innovation is usually labour-saving and tends to originate in industrialized countries, moving toward developing countries like India, Pakistan where labour tends to be low cost and abundant. Would it therefore make sense to slow down or somehow restrict technology transfer, especially to development markets, in the interest of preserving employment?

The answer here is clearly—no. Historical evidence abundantly demonstrates that attempts to retard technological progress bring about grater poverty and lower growth. Technology, in fact, is at the heart of the new endogenous growth theory which is very much in vogue among development economists today. Slowing down or inhibiting technology transfer would certainly dash many countries' development hopes and aggravate poverty. However, the relationship between technology, development, employment and poverty alleviation is not without its complications.

In the 1980s, the buzz word among development specialists was "appropriate technology", i.e., small-scale and labour-intensive technologies that would increase productive output while allowing an equilibrium solution to be found such that the ratio of the productivity of labour to that of capital is proportional to their relative prices. The conditions for this "small is beautiful" approach to technology tended to be best met in agricultural production. However, where manufacturing industry is concerned, the small-is-beautiful approach foundered badly when the only viable technological alternatives proved to be highly capital-intensive.

Development Gap

A wide gap has emerged between developing countries with an inward focus (which tended to be projectionist and pursue policies of import substitution) and those with an outward focus and a policy of pursuing export-led growth. Competing in international markets requires technology that is as good as or better than that found in advanced, industrialized nations. Small, therefore, is not beautiful in the global manufacturing economy where product standards are high and the elasticity of substitution between labour and capital is very limited.

The drive to obtain state-of-the-art technology thus leads to a policy conundrum: it is a pre-condition for success in manufactured exports, but the impulse to compete successfully in this most lucrative sector speeds up the transfer of technology from the developed to the developing world, thus reinforcing the bias toward labour saving equipment in developing countries and accelerating a process that is seen as a source of job loss in the industrialized countries.

Technology and Jobs

Before concluding that modern technology transfer is inimical to employment in developing countries, we have to distinguish clearly between technology's static and dynamic consequences. In a static sense, it is true that highly capital-intensive export industries may not create much employment on a net basis, but the dynamic effects of technology transfer do contribute to economic growth. And growth, in turn, generates multiplier effects in the form of demand, which stimulates ancillary production activities (like food processing or consumer goods) that rely on more labour-intensive technologies.

The problem is that the diffusion and application of technology on a global scale blurs the categories of international product specialisation and creates a much more competitive and conflict-prone international environment.

For example, we have already seen the Asian Tigers move from producing goods such as textiles and processed food to producing hi-tech and value-added consumer durables. This advance is only possible due to the growth of human capital (facilitated by investment and higher incomes) and it leaves production of textiles to other industrializing countries, like Indonesia, the Philippines and now China. But the dynamic comes at the expense of jobs in industrialized regions, like the us and the EC, which lost more than a quarter of their work force in textiles during the 1980s. Inspite of job losses, advanced countries continue to produce textiles, notwithstanding major differences in the hourly wage rates for spinning and weaving and the fact that essentially the same hi tech equipment is being used in most production centres.

Protectionism

What has happened in textiles is happening in other industrial sectors (automobiles, for example) as well. The intense market competition is proving to be a source of trade conflicts, and possibly protectionism, as jobs come under increasing pressure.

For many workers and managers, the benefits of foreign direct investment look increasingly like a zero-sum game for employment, and there is a real risk that the tenuous link between overall growth and employment will break down altogether. It is hardly surprising that we are already seeing negatively affected workers and local businesses clamouring for protection in advanced countries.

Government's Role

The concerned governments are suppose to carry out much of this research. The three initial lines of inquiry follow from three reasonable assumptions about the future.

- First, increase in welfare and consumption subsidies are out; investments in training and human capital are in. How can investments in human capital be directed to positive employment effects? Is it perhaps not time to explore more fully benefit schemes targeting the unemployed and the unskilled poor providing them with the type of subsidies that would enhance their human capital, improve their health and productivity through better nutrition and preventive medicine, and restore the dignity of holding a job?
- Second, given the quasi-inevitability of increased automation in manufacturing, how can other sectors (particularly agriculture and services) be developed to export their long-term potential for employment creation?
- Third, given the inevitable pressures of work and productivity in the global economy, what sort, of alternative institutional arrangements need to evolve with respect to industrial relations, employment and work conditions?

Finding answers to these and other questions will require no small amount of new thinking, but parochialism or a failure of imagination would be fatal flaws in this global era.

The Persistence of Indian Poverty and its Alleviation 17

Poverty has always been with us and for atleast forty years its alleviation has been the professed objective of many strategies to improve the lot of the Indians. But the way in which it has been conceived, however, has been subject to considerable change. Relatively little attention was paid to the development of the poor themselves. Rather, they were portrayed as among the beneficiaries of development in larger systems which were to provide the dynamic force for the elimination of poverty (from the "outside" as it were). Development was principally something that happened to the poor—on a "trickle-down" basis.

The simple assumption that the poor would benefit from general economic growth, without paying any special attention to them, changed somewhat in the late 1950s, when it was perceived that the poor might not automatically benefit from macro-economic development, but that they must benefit if the social stability needed for overall economic growth was to be assured. From this point there emerged a specific line of antipoverty thinking to improve the income of poor people.

The manner is which the poor were to be integrated into the overall growth process, however, was very specific. It was concerned not so much with what the poor could offer to the growth process—as with what they should receive from that process. For all its merits the Basic Needs strategy, and the social "safety net" approach which followed it, basically emphasized the consumption needs of the poor—and not their surplus producing possibilities. On the contrary, a persistent theme in the discourse about the economics of the poor has been the need for some sort of transfer of resources to them from more productive and dynamic sectors of accumulation. In short, the poor have been portrayed as a net burden on the growth process.

It is possible to introduce an element of differentiation into this picture: given that it is rarely alleged that low wages are an obstacle to accumulation and growth, the poor who have been characterized as a burden have tended to be those not directly integrated into nascent large-scale systems of production: these are the poor "peripheral" to modern economic process – a group which encompasses a large proportion of the urban population in India (principally employed in the "informal" sector), as well as a vast mass of small, but relatively independent agricultural producers.

Implicitly, then, the concepts of "peripheral", small-scale and poor have been run together to form, in the realm of ideas, a more or less dependent mass. The number of people ostensibly in these categories is huge, and they seem to represent an enormous burden on development. They represent a development "problem", and an awesome one at that.

While substantial progress has been made in India in reducing the percentage of the rural population below nationally defined poverty line, the absolute number of the rural poor has increased. The growth of output did not bring about a significant improvement in the income share of the lowest nor an uniform reduction in the percentage of the rural population below the poverty line. The situation actually worsened less than half of the rural population in India has access to safe water or sanitation, and only 60 per cent had any access to health services. National data on life expectancy, infant mortality and literacy show improvement, but also the persistence of completely unacceptable conditions.

The pursuit of growth has not solved the development problem. Trickle-down has not worked or it has not worked enough. The massive persistence of poverty, particularly in rural areas represents a problem for the popular acceptance of continued economic adjustment; and it represents a problem for growth itself. The problem lies not only in the unintended consequence of the prevailing development paradigm, but in the viability of the paradigm itself. Part of the debt crisis arose from an inability to mobilize fully domestic assets, and from systematic resort to external resources. The unsustainability of this form of development has been amply demonstrated. Part of the answer to the challenge of development lies in a greater and more appropriate use of the resources of developing countries themselves.

A substantial part of these assets can be created by the poor who have been so marginal to past development efforts. The poverty of a nation and the poverty of people are not as easily separable as was often thought in the past. In many cases, it is difficult to envisage national growth without strong economic development among the poor themselves—not as objects, but as subjects of development. The fact that this is insufficiently perceived is as much an expression of the development of social and economic interests as it is no the development or otherwise of economic theory. Development has frequently been associated with large-scale production and large-scale inputs of capital, and these new social and economic patterns have often defined development in their own image, i.e., in terms of the centrality of large-scale production and accumulation.

Poverty Alleviation

The perspective is not that growth achieved by the better-off will pull the poor out of poverty, but that the mobilisation and enhancement of the resources and activities of the poor themselves can uphold their dignity and free them from the shackles of misery, while at the same time making a vital contribution to overall sustainable growth.

Individually and collectively, the obstacles facing the poor are formidable. They are, however, not insepable. Most of the forces creating poverty are essentially social. They reflects systems of resources allocation that are made by societies, and as such they can be reversed. Pricing policies, credit systems, and social and productive services, which neglect the poor, as well as gender discrimination, are no natural, universal and inevitable facts—and neither is the poverty they give rise to. One of the major obstacles to overcome in fighting poverty is the perception of poverty itself—and of the poor. In this regard, perhaps the most important point is that the poor are not idle, they work. Nobody is simply "poor". In other words, it is not just a state of being. In this regard, "poor" is more aptly used as an adjective rather than as a noun. The rural poor are poor farmers, poor herders and poor fishermen. In short, they are poor producers: their incomes are gained from their work. The answer to poverty lies in creating the conditions for them to earn more from their work. From this perspective, overcoming poverty does not mean less growth, it is a contributor to growth—for it means making the poor more productive. Too often in the past poverty alleviation has been seen as a burden on the economy, as involving a transfer of something for nothing in exchange. It need not be that way: It can be an investment in production, benefiting both poor and the national economy. Poverty has been defined as a production problem, and poverty alleviation as an investment.

Nobody wishes to be poor, and few accept it passively. The poor are rarely without initiative. What they lack are the means of pursuing it. In no small measure, overcoming poverty involves building upon this initiative and will, helping organize cooperation, and providing material support. This support does not have to take the form of handouts. The problem of the poor is not that they cannot handle resources efficiently, but they do not have access to them.

The challenge of creating an institutional framework for credit for the poor is an expression of the general institutional challenge facing poverty alleviation: institutions are not oriented to the poor. Many factors enter into this, ranging from the costs of working with a large number of unorganized people, to the prevalence of myths about the improvidence of the poor, to a simple desire on the part of the better-off to monopolize scarce resources. The answer to this is to create institutional responsiveness, either through introducing demand-led organisation into existing institutions concerned with the poor or through promoting institutions created by the poor themselves. In both cases, participation by the poor is critical. The objective is not only to mobilize the individual initiatives of the poor, but also to mobilize their collective strength and capabilities. As individuals, many of the poor are virtually unreachable. As members of associations and groups they create their own channels for institutional access.

The poor as producer; the poor as credit-worthy handlers of material assistance; the poor as institutional actors—these are not elements of theory, but of practice and experience. Notwithstanding the growing acceptance of the need to do something "about" the poor, not everyone shares this understanding of poverty. As long as the poor are viewed from afar, the myths of poverty and the poor persist. Even those who over reemphasize the need for social "safety nets" and handouts, while ostensibly helping the poor, maintain the image of helplessness, and of the need to do something "for" them. A closer view reveal something very different: tremendous work and initiative on the part of the poor, both based on their desire to do something for themselves. This is not a burden, it is an extraordinary social and economic asset. Again, viewed from a distance, poverty looks overwhelming. The closer view reveals very specific situations of opportunities and needs. These can be responded to—not only through soup kitchens, which should be seen as desirable in addressing emergencies only-but through strengthening the individual and collective means available to the poor to carve out their own path of independence and growth. The dynamics of poverty are reversible, but only in collaboration with the poor themselves.

Precisely because of past neglect of the poor as producers, a neglect involving a failure to involve them in the process of technological development, organisation, and capitalisation, the gap between the current and potential production of the poor is enormous. Investment in the poor is not a loss-making enterprise. Poverty is less a failure of the poor, than a failure of policy-makers to grasp their potential. Far from there being a tradeoff between poverty and growth, the persistence of poverty represents a limit to growth.

Mobilizing and enhancing the ability of the rural poor to expand their own income and contribute to national growth is not simply a process of raising incomes. It involves structural change in economies and societies. It involves helping the poor to position themselves securely within main-line economic processes. This means first increasing and improving their access to land—by land reform, land-titlling, better management and better conservation, supported where necessary by irrigation, new technologies and improved infrastructure. Secondly, it means increasing the productivity and use of rural labour, emphasizing labour intensive technology and better training for new skills. Thirdly, it means making more capital available to the rural poor, mobilizing savings, providing infrastructure and developing financial services tailored to their situation and needs.

Not least, it mean acknowledging the important contribution of poor women in all of these areas of activity. At present, the contribution of women to the rural economy is seriously underestimated—the "invisible women" syndrome. Official statistics rarely make any effort to measure it, even though it is more than clear that not just unpaid household work but the farm and trading activities of women make a vital and significant contribution to the well being of poor rural households. All the evidence suggests that the poorer the household the more hour's women work and the greater their investment in both economic production and family welfare. From a situation of multiple disadvantage as poor, as women and often as single parents, women can move to one in which they contribute and benefit three-fold—in the home, in society at large and, not least, in the development of the next generation.

Many of the measure that needs to be taken to allow the poor to realize their potential do not involve more expenditure: they involve the elimination of economic distortions against the rural poor. These distortions have effectively taxed the poor, and mainly the rural poor, in favour of inappropriate and inefficient urban developments whose support has been at the root of widespread economic crises. To no small extent, helping the poor make their potential contribution to development involves no more than creating a "level playing field" and, when conceived in such a light, structural adjustment can make a vital contribution to both resumed growth and social equity. It is often felt that the poor are somehow "outside" the scope of national economic policies. This is virtually never the case. They are affected by national economic policies, but this inclusion takes a very special form: exposure to the costs, and exclusion from the benefits. In this regard, there is a certain irony in the view that small-scale producers "need" subsidies to survive. In fact it has been the development of large-scale production in agriculture (and industry) in India that has been heavily dependent upon subsidisation over the decades—benefits, which smaller-scale producers have rarely enjoyed.

This is characteristic of many forms of large-scale production in India—although nominally at the cutting edge of efficiency and productivity; it is they rather than the small-scale producers who have been dependent upon transfers and protection for their reproduction.

Change in the environment of poverty necessitates greater awareness of the root causes of poverty on the part of policy-makers. However, the realisation of the social and economic potential of the rural poor is not just a question of economic policy and investment. It also involves the development of a general social framework in which the economic and social interests of the poor can be freely articulated and responded to. It means instilling democratic and participatory values at every level in society and not just at the level of nationwide institutions. The most valid spokesmen of the poor are the poor themselves.

The opening of economic and social opportunities to the poor offers the possibility of more stable and sustainable change. The alternative is for societies to polarize further, for the welfare burden to grow to greater proportions and for a widening gap to develop between the modern and traditional sectors. In the end, the continued poverty of the rural areas will be a brake on the output of the advanced sector, eroding the potential for self-sustaining growth.

Overcoming the Poverty in India and the Lessons Learned 18

Basic elements in the struggle against poverty in India are the provision of the economic services and assets, which the poor have tended not to receive in the past—as a result of oversight or design. The emphasis on economic services and assets is just because the mass of the rural poor are self-employed, and it is upon the improvement in the means of production directly accessible to them that their prosperity depends. Health and education are very important, but offer more if combined with the material means of making a living—of putting body and mind to work. These assets and services include land, water, technology, commercial services, handling output and inputs, and credit-provided within an economic policy famework conductive to their optimal exploitation.

This list is hardly new. It corresponds to the requirements of any producer. The basic points to be made in this regard are: firstly, that the general requirements of poor producers are precisely the same as those of other producer and that measures to alleviate poverty that fall short of recognizing the full range of such requirements are doomed to failure; and, secondly, that these assets and services are not typically provided in a form accessible to the poor. India has made important progress in providing a more effective framework for agricultural production "in general", this framework has not properly embraced small and poor producers. They are as follows:

Access to Land and Water

In the case of access to land, for example, land reform efforts in India has frequently involved major loop-holes, allowing the socially powerful to minimize de facto improvements in the condition of the poor. In the critical area of land rights, registration processes have been so complex and costly relative to the resources of the poor that land regularization programmes have, sometimes unintentionally, become virtual characters for legalizing the eviction of the poor and the actual loss of their traditional rights. Irrigation without specific measures to defend the interests of existing occupants of areas exposes them to expulsion—and, moreover, has tended to be concentrated in large-scale schemes benefiting already high potential areas in which the better off predominate. While huge sums have been spent on large-scale irrigation schemes, little has been spent on water conservation and the sort of small-scale developments that are more likely to be of relevance to marginal small-scale producers.

Technology Transfer

In the area of technology, attention has been focused on technologies (such as the Green Revolution) requiring extensive access to water and fertilizers, neither of which are generally available among the poor. In fact, research almost every-where has concentrated on larger-scale production in areas of relatively high resource endowment. In contrast to this, research relevant to small-scale producers in marginal soil and rainfed areas in India has been shockingly deficient. As in other fields, this is partly explicable in terms of a frequently unproved belief that large-scale production is more efficient. It is also explicable in terms of the fact that it is the powerful who set the research agenda, not the poor. Taking its inspiration from highly specialized, large-scale agricultural units of production, research has tended to dwell separately on individual crops—rather than on the interaction between crops, which is of much greater relevance to small-scale producers engaging in highly complex systems of production to maximize food self-sufficency and minimize risks.

Commercial Services

In the area of handling of output an inputs, organized services (not infrequently under public control in the past) have tended to concentrate in the proximity of large-scale producers and users of input in relatively well-endowed areas. In India the poor have had to incur the extraordinary costs of handling their own transport of good to and from service points—frequently over long and deficient lines of communication. The alternative has been to resort to private intermediaries offering goods, and buying products, at prices very different from those enjoyed by larger producers. In effect, the better-off and the poor have confronted different sets of prices—with the poor paying more for what they buy, and receiving less for what they sell.

Credit

In the area of credit, the situation has been disastrous. It is generally recognised that productive improvement needs a change in means of production—new tools, improved seeds, fertilizers, etc. Such a change everywhere is typically effected on the basis of credit. Yet rural credit schemes in India have usually not extended support to small farmers and the poor. Credit has been concentrated among richer farmers with collateral and with demand for larger loans. In order to improve their productivity, the poor have been forced to seek credit from informal money lenders—at virtually confiscatory rates. Again, the cost of modernization has been much higher for the poor than for the better-off. The inevitable result has been a lower rate of change—and the consolidation, rather than the reduction of poverty.

The Victims Blamed

Although vast amounts of money have been invested in rural development in India, very little of it has reached the poor. The have been left to their own devices, while the better-off have received a wide range of assistance—not infrequently allowing them to encroach further upon the land of the poor. Support for agricultural expansion has not led to rural development, and it has not eliminated rural poverty. The relatively undynamic performance of many small-scale farmers under these circumstances is frequently taken as "proof" that they are a poor investment. This is a variant of "blaming the victim". In fact, the poor have fared badly, not because they could not efficiently use support, but because they did not get it.

In other words, the failure of the poor to benefit from agricultural sector investments has not reflected an economic failure among the poor themselves. Rather, it has involved policy and institutional failures. On the policy level, it has tended to reflect an unwillingness to restrain the socially influential from seeking to monopolize scarce resources to their own benefit—and, perhaps, a lack of awareness of the incompatibility between apparently "netural" criteria for support (e.g., the demand for land title as collateral for credit) and the particular circumstances of poor and small farmer (e.g., involvement) in traditional forms of land tenure). On the institutional level, it has involved both unwillingness to give weight to the requirements of the poor, and a lack of initiative in solving real problems in providing services to the poor such as the high cost of providing services on an individual basis to a large number of small and often dispersed "clients". While there has been a great deal of lamentation about poverty in India, remarkably little has been done to change it at the level of economic systems—perhaps because social welfare activities are much easier to implement than real policy and institutional changes. It is possible to do very much better—not by simply pouring in more resources (in channels which at times do not even ultimately reach the poor), but by changing the framework of investment, i.e., the instruments of development.

LESSONS LEARNED

Targeting of Resources

The fundamental lessons learned are that investment resources must be targeted at the poor. In a world of competition for scarce resources, investments in rural development tend to be captured by those with national and local power—a group, which rarely encompasses the rural poor. The first step in delivering resources to the poor is establishing strict criteria for eligibility for assistance. Indicators of wealth in India vary according to the nature of the local economy—in some cases it is extent of land ownership, in others size of cattle herds, in yet others ownership of draught animals—but the principle remains the same: investment in those with the least assets. In some cases, for example, where women represent a significant proportion of actual producers, this may give rise to entirely new patterns of investment.

Reorienting Institutions

The intention to distribute resources to the poorest is not always accompanied by actual performance. Among the reasons for this is the inappropriateness of delivery mechanisms. Put simply, institutions long oriented to the non-poor have tended to develop operating procedures and structures which reflect the nature of their de facto clientele and which hinder them from serving a new target group. In the area of credit, for example, insistence upon collateral in land may be an absolute obstacle to participation by the poor—just as a limited banking network may represent an obstacle to delivery to the poor, for who the costs of communicating with a bank at considerable distance might well add significantly to the real cost of credit. Effectively channeling resources to the poor, therefore, means the elaboration of institutional means of delivery consistent with their circumstances.

However, it must be recognized that there are exceptional institutional costs associated with providing services to (and among) the poor-costs arising from the fact that there are many individuals involved, and that their individual requirements tend to be quite small. The costs of government services in, for example, agricultural credit, are necessarily higher if this involves a very large number of small producers than if it involves a small number of large producers. Administration costs in banking tend to be much higher relative to loan volume if it involves a myriad of individual small loans. These factors have often, been adduced as reasons for the "impossibility" of serving the poor. Effective Service appears financially impossible, especially the context of widespread retrenchment in public expenditure under structural adjustment programmes. The poor are often willing to pay the actual costs of services—especially if the alternative is no service at all, or supply by local informal monopolists. On the other hand, there are proven ways of reducing costs of service supply to the poor—by involving the poor themselves. Everywhere in India poor people overcome some of the obstacles involved in their individual poverty through cooperation and joint action. While such organization typically develops in the absence of formal service organizations and markets, it can also develop in association with formal organizations. In effect, the organized small farmer can help shoulder the cost of services through organizing local level distribution and administration themselves.

People's Participation

People's participation is, therefore, not only a "social" concept. It is an eminently economic concept, involving cost sharing. It is fundamental to the sustainability of improvements. The long-term solution is not to throw money at the problems of the poor, but to help them to organize to overcome them themselves. One of the happy externalities of this approach is not only lower cost services, but services more likely to be in harmony with what small farmers perceive themselves as needing.

Balanced Development

Development means change, not only in the volume of production, but in the composition of output and the conditions under which it is produced. What is argued is that the pursuit of development without the inclusion of the mass of small-scale producers and the poor has important structural drawbacks, and that their inclusion offers the basis for more sustainable long-term development. Some smallholder groups have a vast unutilized potential for expansion. Others have much more modest prospects.

Even those with the poorest assets and possibilities however, can be helped to improve their condition. While the direct economic benefits of this maybe relatively slender, the side-effects may be great. An eventual shift of these groups to other areas and systems of production might be inevitable if aspiration for a better life are to be satisfied, but it is essential that this shift be orderly necessitating that support be given in the transitional period. This support can be either a direct welfare transfer or an investment in productive capacity. In many cases the latter may be the least-coast alternative.

The issue, then, is neither the "rich way" nor the "poor way". What is required is: an unprejudiced evaluation of the capacities and possibilities of poor and small-scale producers, and their potential role in the overall scheme of national development; allocation of investment resources according to potential and within an institutional framework ensuring delivery and profitable use; and a more balanced view of the overall social costs land benefits of alternative means of addressing transitional states. The belief is that the outcome of this will involve a reappraisal of the role of the poor in economic development, and a major improvement in the state of the rural poor throughout India.

Population Growth and Jobs 19

Since mid-century, the world's labour force has more than doubled-from 1.2 billion people to 2.7 billion, outstripping the growth in job creation. As a result, the United Nations International Labour Organisation estimates that nearly 1 billion people, approximately 30 per cent of the global work force, are unemployed or underemployed (working but not earning enough to meet basic needs). Over the next half—century, the world will need to create more than 1.9 billion jobs-all of them in the developing world—just to maintain current levels of employment.

As economists often note, while population growth may boost labour demand (through economic activity and demand for goods), it will most definitely boost labour supply. During the next 50 years, almost 40 million people will enter the global labour force—defined as those between the ages of 15 and 65 seeking work-each year. Between 1995 and 2050, some 1.9 billion additional jobs will need to be created to absorb these new would be workers. The most pressing needs will be found in the world's poorest nations—a sobering example of the vicious cycle linking poverty and population growth.

As the children of today represent the workers of tomorrow, the interaction between population growth and jobs is most acute in nations with young populations. Nations such as Peru, Mexico, Indonesia, and Zambia with more than half their population below the age of 25 will feel the burden of this labour flood. In the Middle East and Africa, 40 per cent of the population is under the age of 15. Since new entrants into the labour force were born at least 15 years ago, measures to reduce population growth have a delayed effect on the growth of the labour force, highlighting the urgency of taking action on population.

Nowhere is the employment challenge grater than in Africa, where at least 40 per cent of the population lives in absolute poverty. Although 8 million people entered the sub-Saharan work force in 1997, by 2030 this resource-scarce region will have to absorb more than 17 million new entrants each year. Over the next half-century, Nigeria's labour force is projected to grow by 246 per cent and Ethiopia's will soar by 337 per cent—both faster than growth of the general population. At current growth rates, the size of the labour force in sub-Saharan Africa will more than triple by 2050.

As a result of unprecedented population growth and increasing acceptance of female participation in the work force, the number of people seeking jobs in the Middle East and North Africa, a region already plagued by double-digit unemployment rates, will double in the next 50 years. In Algeria, where unemployment stands at 22 per cent, the labour force is growing at a staggering 4.2 per cent annually, and the number seeking work will more than double by 2050. Egypt alone will need to create 26 million more jobs by 2050 as its total population hits 115 million.

Nations throughout Asia will also see phenomenal increases in the numbers seeking work, including Pakistan, where the work force will grow from 70 million in 1998 to 205 million by 2050. Over the next 25 years, India will add nearly 10 million to its work force each year. During the same period, China will add nearly 6 million annually due to population growth alone, compounding the work shortages caused by the current flood of migrants to China's coastal cities and by massive layoffs—estimated at more than 30 million—as state-run operations are scaled back.

Nations are hard-pressed to educate and train rapidly growing numbers of young people in marketable skills for the global workplace. Moreover, meeting the basic needs of a growing population draws scarce foreign exchange and other resources from investments in education and job creation. Throughout the world, young people entering the work force are increasingly faced with unemployment and social marginalisation. In most societies, unemployment rates for those under 25 are substantially higher than for older people.

Surplus farmland once served as a traditional source of employment for growing populations, as new land could be ploughd to generate work and income. However, global percapita Greenland has dropped by half and considerably more in certain nations since 1950. Moreover, the machanisation of agriculture fuels the exodus of job seekers into the world's urban areas, where unemployment is often most acute heavily reliant on natural capital in the past, future job creation will require massive amounts of financial capital to jump-start the industrial and service sectors.

As the balance between the demand and supply of labour is tipped by population growth, wages—the price of labour—tend to decrease. And in a situation of labour surplus, the quality of jobs may not improve as fast for workers will settle for longer hours, fewer benefits and less control over work activities.

Employment is the key to obtaining food, housing, health services, and education, in addition to providing self-respect and self-fulfilment. Rising numbers of unemployed people could drive global poverty and hunger to precarious levels, fuelling political instability.

Living with Leviathan 20

In the year 2015, there will mega-cities with more than 8 million inhabitants—22 of them in Asia. How will they cope? Humanity is about to set a new record. Nearly two-thirds of the planet's population will be living in cities by 2025, UN population expert say. Until now, rural people have outnumbered city-dwellers.

World population, according to the same projections, will top eight billion in 25 year's time, including five billion in cities. The increase will be particularly spectacular in the cities of the developing world. Whose total population will double to four billion. We are going to see an unprecedented exodus of people from rural areas.

The demographer's predictions are only tentative of course. But the flow of people into megacities in developing countries is well under way. Several sociological changes are behind it.

Cities used to need muscle-power for the jobs they provided, the experts point out. But today they no longer attract people just because of their economic potential. There's plenty of evidence that they can go on steadily attracting people even when the job-generating sectors are in bad shape or disappearing.

People no longer move to urban centres because they are fairly sure to find work. They do so because they want to leave the countryside where there are too many people tilling the land and because they hope to leave poverty behind. Rightly or wrongly, the city seems to offer progress and freedom, a vision of opportunity, an irresistible lure.

The result is that both inside and outside cities, there are more and more squatters and poor housing. Urbanisation in the developing world differs from that in the industrialized countries, in "the speed of the process, the growth of poverty, the extent of urban sprawl and the expansion of the informal economy."

How are the authorities in the developing world's urban areas responding to such "invasions"? In today's deregulated world, the trend is to question the very idea of providing the general population with basic urban services, most observers note. For want of resources, cities in developing countries are increasingly abandoning their public service function.

China is still an exception to this in several ways. Officials there, in a context of rigid planning—though this has eased in recent year—are trying to prevent the influx of more rural migrants than the city economies can cope with as the example of Shanghai show. Can such a policy, which works fairly well for the moment, survive the political and economic hangs underway?

At the other end of the scale is Lagos (Nigeria), whose expansion is chaotic. About 200 slums have sprung up in this African city. Every now and then, one of them is bulldozed without notice and without heed for its inhabitants. But Lagos survives thanks to the vibrant ingenuity of its millions of citizens. Another revealing city is Jakarta, where the authorities themselves have joined in frantic property speculation. As a result of this speculation, more than 4.5 million people have been evicted from their homes in the last 30 years, with little compensation, to make possible the construction of high-rise blocks, which sometimes stand empty

How do the original inhabitants of a city react to the massive influx of people from outside? In more and more cities, you see smart neighbourhood protected by guards—called "fortress-cities". In these fortified enclaves, built partly in response to real or imagined lack of security, the road, sewage system, schools and other community services are private. Outside them, public areas have been abandoned to the least fortunate members of the society and the infrastructure there is crumbling or inadequate. The middle and poorer classes also defend themselves in their own neighbourhoods. One surprising case can be found in the satellite cities just outside Brasilia, where iron railings protect the houses, from fancy villas to the humblest shack.

Will the mega-cities of the 21st century be made up of island of "social tribes"- "anticities" of walled enclaves, who's wealthy residents refuse to pay taxes to provide facilities for the city's less fortunate inhabitants? Will cities still integrate their inhabitants?

"The existence of a slum mean the authorities have failed." Says the World Bank. The bank encourages projects where the state and the private sector join hands to help the less fortunate buy plots of land in areas with an infrastructure. Other experts say the "anti-social" aspects of globalisation should be blamed. They would like to see the big cities of the next century return to their original function as a across road and a meeting-place.

Population Growth and Education 21

In contrast to the food supply challenge posed by the coming wave of population growth, the global need for teachers and classrooms will rise very slowly in the next half-century. In many countries, the school-age population is increasing much less rapidly than the overall national population. The trend illustrates that growth rates typically differ for different age strata of the population. It also shows that declining birth rates can take decades to move through an entire population.

At the global level, for example, total population is projected to increase by 54 per cent between 2000 and 2050, but the number of children aged 5 to 14 will grow by only 6 per cent. And of the world's largest countries—accounting for 60 per cent of global population in 1995—will actually begin to see decreases in the number of children aged 5 to 14 by 2015; for several of these countries, the decline in this age group has already begun. These countries will need fewer classrooms and teachers to educate the youngest members of society (assuming they maintain current class size and student-teacher ratios).

Plenty of nations, however, still have increasing child-age populations. Where countries have not acted to stabilize population, the base of the national population pyramid continues to expand, and pressures on the educational system will be severe. In the world's 10 fastest-growing countries, for example, most of which are in Africa and the Middle East, the child-age population will increase in average 93 per cent over the next half-century. Africa as a whole will see its school-age population grow by 75 per cent through 2040.

The rapid growth in African populations is especially worrisome because of the extra burden it imposes in a region already lagging in education. Only 56 per cent of Africans south of the Sahara are literate, compared with 71 per cent for all developing countries. Few African countries have universal primary education, and secondary education reaches only 4-5 per cent of African children. Educating today's children is challenge enough; the addition of another three students for every four already there will require heroic investments in education. But the alternatives is grim: without additional investments in education, today's average student-teacher ratio of 42 in sub-Saharan Africa will reach 75 by 2040.

Many countries will be challenged to increase funding for education while ensuring that other worthy sectors also receive the support they need. With 900 million illiterate adults in the world, the case for a renewed commitment to education is easy to make. But competiting for these funds are the 840 million chronically hungry and the 1.2 billion without access to a decent toilet.

The budget stresses on governments attempting to meet these basic needs would clearly be reduced with smaller populations. Mozambique and Lesotho, for example, both met the UNESCO benchmark for investment in education in 1992—6 per cent of gross domestic product—and the two countries economies were roughly equal in size. Yet because Mozambique has many times the population of Lesotho, spending per child in Lesotho is about nine times higher than in Mozabique. For the majority of countries who do not meet the UNESCO funding standard, many of whom also fall short in providing other basic services, a decline in population pressure could help substantially to meet all of their social goals.

If national education systems begin to stress life-long learning for a rapidly changing world, as recommended by a 1998 UNESCO report on education in the twenty-first century, then extensive provision for adult education will be necessary, affecting even those countries with shrinking childgage populations, such a development means that countries that started population stabilisation programmes earliest will be in the best position to educate their entire citizenry.

Population Growth and Housing 22

Over the past half-century, the world's housing stock has grown roughly in step with population. Yet for more and more people worldwide, adequate and affordable housing remains beyond reach, driving some into substandard dwellings and slums and others onto the street. This situation stands to worsen, for the need for housing worldwide is projected to nearly double over the next 50 years.

Although industrial nations currently occupy a disproportionately large share of the world's households relative to their population, virtually all future growth will occur in developing countries, where housing requirements will more than double by the middle of the twenty-first century. This phenomenal growth results from the potent synergy between population growth and a shift toward fewer people per household—a trend that is especially pronounced where economic growth is rapid.

HABITAT, the United Nations Centre for Human Settlements, has projected housing requirements based on roughly a 30-per cent reduction in people per household over the next 50 years. These figures are purely statistical estimates and do not consider possible checks in housing growth, such as materials or financial constraints, intensified land competition, or increased poverty. Our own projections assume that household size will indeed decrease, as fertility rates drop and as extended families become more rare, but by a more modest 15 per cent.

Over the next 50 years, housing needs in Africa and the Middle East are expected to increase more than threefold, with tremendous gains in the region's most populous nations; demands are to increase 3.5 times in Nigeria and 4.5 times in Ethiopia. Although less dramatic percentage increases are expected in Asia, the doubling of households in the region will require nearly 700 million additional homes by 2050. Still, some countries there, such as Pakistan and neighbouring Afghanistan, will see housing needs increase nearly three and a half times.

The projected growth in housing needs becomes all the more daunting given that rapid population growth—combined with rapid urban growth—has already left a large share of the world's population without adequate housing. HABITAT estimates that at least 600 million urban dwellers and more than 1 billion rural dwellers in Africa, Asia, and Latin America live in housing that is so overcrowded and of such poor quality with such inadequate provision for water, sanitation, drainage, and garbage collection that their lives and their health are continually at risk.

As the supply of housing falls behind demand, the quality of available housing tends to deteriorate. Cheaper, less durable materials, such as scrap metal and cardboard, are substituted for more expensive, weather-resistant materials, such as concrete and wood. Fierce competition in swelling urban areas for desirable land can eliminate all hope of low-income households acquiring a plot for housing. As choice of location dwindles, shantytowns and other low-quality settlements develop on marginal land ill suited for housing—in floodplains, on steep hillsides, near garbage dumps or others environmentally risky sites. From New York to Beijing, cities are faced with land and materials constraints even as their populations continue to grow.

At the same time, housing area per person continues to increase in certain nations and among the more affluent segments of other nations, placing additional stress on prime space and building materials. In the United States, Western Europe, and Japan—a nation traditionally known for small dwellings—floor space per person has more than doubled in new single family homes since mid-century. The global disparity in floor space per person—Washington, D.C., at the high end with 70 square metres per person, and most of humanity at around

9 square metres per person—will likely mimic the growing global disparity in income, as wealthy household scale up and poorer households fill up.

Housing can provide a connection to a supply of fresh water and sanitation facilities. But as its quality deteriorates, so do these basic amenities. Half the world's people are without access to sanitation and nearly this many—2.7 billion—are without a reliable source of safe drinking water. Shortages of housing that provides these basic services are most acute in cities, where rapid urbanisation and high population densities place heightened demands on infrastructure. And still housing needs are projected to soar in the regions of the world where access to water and sanitation are most constrained.

The ultimate manifestation of population growth outstripping the supply of housing is homelessness. The United Nations estimates that a least 100 million of the world's people-roughly the same as the population of Mexico have no home; the number tops 1 billion if those with especially insecure or temporary accommodations, such as squatters, are included. In many developing countries, squatter communities are home to 30-60 per cent of the urban population. There are some 250, 000 pavement dwellers in Bombay alone. Humans who are born, live, and die in the streets—are common in all major cities. Unless the world moves to a lower population trajectory, the ranks of homeless are likely to swell dramatically.

23 Children's Health and the Environment

Children today live in an environment vastly different from that of a few generations ago. Economic development, increased urbanisation and the consequences of war in many countries have added to the traditional environmental hazards, those problems associated with environmental pollution. Thus, while some traditional children's diseases such as diarrhoea, malnutrition and infectious diseases persist in many countries, environmentally-related illnesses such as asthma, respiratory illness due to environmental tobacco smoke (ETS), as well as mortality and morbidity due to injuries, are increasing. In childhood cancer in some countries and the potential risks of endocrine-disrupting chemicals are among the emerging health threats that need careful vigilance. Children of lower socio-economic status are likely to suffer disproportionately from all these threats as a consequence of living in highly polluted environment, poor quality housing, lower levels of education, and of restricted access to environmental and health care services.

Children's Vulnerability

The concern for children's vulnerability to environmental health threats is based on several factors. Children receive greater exposures than adults do because they drink more water, eat more food and have higher breathing rates per unit of body weight. Because they are undergoing rapid growth and development, toxicant effects at specific times may have irreversible consequences. For example, if vital connections between nerve cells fail to form during brain development, there is high risk that the resulting neurobehavioural dysfunction will be permanent and irreversible. Also, because most children have more future years of life than adults, they have more time to develop any chronic disease that may be triggered by early environmental exposures.

Public Health Threats

Asthma, injuries, and the effects of environmental tobacco smoke (ETS) are among the most significant public health threats to children. Childhood asthma is increasingly prevalent in all most of all countries. What causes asthma is not known, but several environmental factors, such as indoor air quality (particularly exposure to the house-dust mite) and ETS, have been linked with the increase in asthma. In addition, outdoors air pollutants such as particulates; sulphur dioxide and ozone exacerbate asthma symptoms. ETS, especially smoking by the mother, is a known risk factor for asthma. ETS is also known to cause acute and chronic middle ear disease and is associated with sudden infant death syndrome (SIDS).

Potential for Prevention

The variation in asthma and injury rates and the evidence of the role of certain environmental factors underline the potential for prevention. Public policies should seek to avoid preventable childhood diseases by preventing exposures to environmental agents and considering children's characteristics and susceptibilities in the development of environmental health legislation. Promoting citizen awareness and participation in policy-making through education and access to environmental information are important elements in achieving a safe environment for children. In this context, children are not only consumers with rights, but also citizens who can play an active role towards their own protection.

International Awareness

Several international agreements have acknowledged children's vulnerabilities and have committed their signatories to protect children's health form the effects of a deteriorating environment. This year, many countries will address several of the environmental health threats to children through international and national action. It is expected that a large international collaborative initiative will result under the guidance of WHO and other international organisations.

24 Land Tenure: *Securing Land for the Urban Poor*

Around the world, especially in Asia and Africa, towns and cities are expanding rapidly. For the poorest people, finding affordable, safe and secure urban land for shelter has become increasingly difficult. This is because:

- Overall competition for land makes it increasingly costly:
- Central urban areas are being developed for commercial use;
- Natural features such as mountains or swamps limit physical urban expansion; and
- Meeting land management and planning standards (concerned with legality, technical and administrative accuracy) is expensive.
- As a result, a large and increasing proportion of urban populations are forced to live in peripheral areas or occupy marginalised and dangerous locations. These settlements are often illegal and, providing inadequate shelter and lacking essential services only exacerbate the problems of the poor. Higher levels of ill health, unemployment and non-sustainable land-use often result. Furthermore, residents may also be under constant threat of eviction by government and exploitation by landowners.

Experience shows that, if residents in such areas feel secure and safe from eviction, they do over time improve their neighbourhoods. Recognition of and granting of secure forms of tenure to previously illegal settlements often provides the incentive to communities to invest their resources in upgrading their housing and wider neighbourhoods. Security of tenure also brings the improved likelihood of basic infrastructure and other essential community services.

There is wide range of urban land tenure systems. In many urban areas, including areas designated illegal by government, there are informal or customary tenure systems—these are often the commonest form of tenure and are expanding most rapidly.

While statutory or "legal" forms of tenure (for example freehold or leasehold agreements) offer many advantages, such as full individual rights and security and access to formal credit systems, they can also cause the very problems they were intended to solve:

- Higher rental levels, which may displace existing renters;
- The selling out of the secure land to higher income groups
- Encouragement of new illegal/informal settlements, as the poorest hope that they will also eventually get security of tenure;
- Encouragement of landowners and developers to hold land, without investing in its improvement or paying taxes on it increased value—which serves to attract even greater levels of investment and land price inflation.
- In addition, if people's incomes remain low and the capacity of the banks or credit unions is weak, statutory forms of tenure alone may not necessarily stimulate neighbourhood improvements.

Consequently, careful analysis of existing systems of informal and customary tenure and property right is required, before embarking on major land management and tenure reforms. These can provide both acceptable levels of security and access to credit, which in turn stimulate improvements to local neigbourhoods. Before any decisions are made, tenure policies must recognise the likely impact on tenants, the poor and other vulnerable groups, especially women.

For these reasons, it is sometimes better to increase the rights of resident (e.g. by protecting them from the threat of forced evictions, or by increasing their access to essential utilities or credit), rather than assuming that they need freehold or leasehold titles.

Strategies for providing shelter now recognise the diverse nature of needs, and the positive contribution which decent housing makes to social and economic development at both national and local levels. They also recognise that the most effective way of mobilising the resources required is to encourage investment in housing by individuals, communities and the private sector.

Recent experience shows that many governments are now introducing positive approaches, which are market-sensitive and encourage more efficient use of available land. These include measures to encourage landowners and developers to allocate a specified proportion of units to low-income groups out of profits generated from planning permission granted by (and therefore partly created by) the government. Public-private partnerships and revisions to planning standards and administrative procedures have also demonstrated that it is possible to reduce the costs of access to land for the poor even under conditions of market-led development, thus reducing urban sprawl, the occurrence of slum settlements and levels of poverty.

City Politics: *A Voice for the Poor* 25

By 2020 the world's urban population will rise by almost 1.5 billion. Cities and towns house a growing proportion of poor people, partly because of the increased share of urban population of the total but also because economic recession and adjustment policies often hit poorer urban residents the hardest. Cities are associated with economic growth and wealth generation and yet inequality is high. Poor people generally live in substandard conditions, may not benefit from job creation, and suffer high levels of pollution, crime and violence.

How can city governments cope with the challenges of population growth and increased global economic competition, and meet the needs of poor residents/is urban governance responsive to the needs of the poor? Are the agencies responsible for city government, especially the municipalities, addressing poor people's needs? Are NGOs and people's organisations playing a greater role in service delivery? Or is their role one of advocacy and lobbying? If so, how do they relate to the formal political system? Can governments fulfil their responsibilities, including poverty reduction? How can the well being of poor urban governance institutions prioritise their needs? In assessing the responsiveness of city government to poor people, three key questions are addressed:

How can the Poor Influence the Agenda of the Institutions of Urban Governance?

The influence of poor residents on decision making is controlled, in part, by the formal political system. Democratisation gives people a vote. However, this vote means more when elected representatives depend on the political support of poor people—where they are a majority, or are well organised, or where there is a ward-based system. If poor people are organised enough, to articulate their needs and demand a fair share of urban resources. NGOs can help poor groups organise better and provide support for networking.

Where poor people are not organised it does not mean they are politically powerless. Poor people in this situation, however, are prey to the disadvantages of patronage and unlikely to be included in formal consultative processes. For an electoral system to be truly responsive, specific mechanisms and channels, such as consultative and participatory processes at city an sub-city levels, are needed to complement representative democracy. Athough. These channels do not necessarily include the poorest or make a marked difference to resource allocation, pro-poor decisions are unlikely without them.

How Can Cities Finance their Activities and Reduce Poverty?

Democratisation has not, in many countries brought allocation of financial resources or the revenue-raising capacity for local governments to fulfil their responsibilities. The responsiveness of city governments to poor people's needs thus depends, on whose voices are heard in the arenas of political decision-making. Responsiveness also depends on how available financial resources are allocated and how the programmes they finance are designed. There is scope, for city governments to increase property and business revenues, and to borrow for capital investment. Whether increased financial resources benefit poor people depends on how the demands of external investors and creditors are reconciled with the demands of poor residents; the willingness of politicians and officials to address the distributive implications of existing and planned spending; and efficient transparent financial management. If funds are made available to sub-city levels of government or if expenditure can be influenced by ward councillors, the funds might then be used to meet the priorities of poor residents.

What are the Necessities of Urban Living and how can Access to them be Ensured?

An adequate income: Work opportunities should be the top priority. City governments can, however, support the urban economy in general and the economic activities of the poor in particular. Firstly they can ensure that the basic services are efficiently provided. Secondly city governments can refrain from activities that destroy the assets and livelihoods of the poor, especially eviction of informal settlements and micro-enterprises. Savings and credit schemes can be more appropriately organised at a community level and supported by NGOs.

Land Ownership is a common aspiration for poor households. A home with secure tenure (not necessarily title) provides security, an appreciating asset, access to services, and a base for economic activities. Increasing the opportunities for poor households to gain access to a well-located plot of land is an important component of any poverty reduction strategy. Many never fulfil their dream and the needs of those who cannot, or do not wish to become home owners should not be neglected, however.

Local government is potentially more responsive to poor residents than are central government agencies, although this depends on the balance of political power and bureaucratic perceptions. The limited ability of the public sector to secure benefits for the poor from public-private partnerships in land development, suggest that more informal arrangements and the involvement of CSOs may be better ways forward.

Environmental Services: Land alone will not reduce poverty but must be linked to a healthy living environment—a package of appropriate and affordable environmental services, such as public transport, water and sanitation, solid waste collection, and energy for cooking and lighting. Rather than discussing appropriate standards, detailed issues of financing and affordability or how continued provision can be assured for each of these services, the research focused on how far decision making channels. Mechanisms and partnership arrangements ensure that providers are responsive to the needs and priorities of poor residents.

Collaborative planning and decision making arrangements are one promising alternative, despite, the current shortcomings of participatory budgeting. For responsiveness to the poor to be built in to such processes, local bureaucrats need to change their attitudes and working practices. Is it possible and acceptable for poor people to have to rely on their own resources their households and networks-resources that are very limited? Informal networks and links can, however, provide mutual support and access to politicians and bureaucrats, community associations though not always present, inclusive or transparent, can play an important role in articulating poor residents views and in organising self-help activities. There is scope for formal representative community organisations, for informal links between peoples' organsiations and the power structures, and for networking between people's groups. NGOs can play an important role in developing the capacity of community organisations and in facilitating networking. Where NGOs play a role in service delivery. However, there is a danger that the resulting close relationship with local government detracts from their ability to empower poor people and challenge inappropriate policies. City governments, it is clear, cannot cope with the challenges of population and economic growth and respond to the needs of poor people alone. Only in alliance with other actors is there some hope that poverty can be overcome. For CSOs, many of which were forged during struggles for democratisation, this implies moving beyond confrontation to engagement. To form alliances between CSOs and city governments that put the interests of the poor first, poor people must be able to exercise their political rights.

Bibliography

Agarwal, Bina. 1992. "Gender Relations and Food Security: Coping with Seasonality, Drought and Famine in South Asia." In Lourdes Beneria and Shelley Feldman, eds. *Unequal Burden: Economic Crises, Persistent Poverty, and Women's Work.* Boulder, Colo.: Westview Press.

Agarwal, Bina. 1997. "Bargaining and Gender Relations: Within and Beyond the Household." *Feminist Economics* 3(1): 1-51.

Akerlof, Geogre, A., and Rachel E. Kranton, 1999. *Economic and Identity.* Washington, D.C.: Brookings Institute.

Alkire, Sabina. 1999," Operationalizing Amartya Sen's Capability Approach to Human Development: A Framework for Identifying 'Valuable' Capabilites." Ph. D. diss, Oxford University.

Baulch, Bob. 1996a. "Neglected Trade-Offs in Poverty Measurement." *IDS Bulletin* 27(1): 36-42.

Baulch, Bob. 1996b. "The New Poverty Agenda: A Disputed Consensus." *IDS Bulletin* 27(1): 1-10.

Bebbington A., and T. Perreault. 1999. "Social Capital, Development and Access to Resources in Highland Ecuador." *Economic Geography* October.

Beneria, Lourdes, 1989. "Gender and the Global Economy." In Arthur MacEwan and William Tabb, eds. *Instability and Change in the Global Economy.* New York: Monthly Review Press.

Berelson, Bernard. 1954. "Content Analysis," *Handbook of Social Psychology.* Vol. 1 Reading, Mass; Addision-Wesley.

Bhatt, Mihir. 1999. "Natural Disasters as National Shocks to the Poor and Development," Disaster Mitigation Institute, Ahmedabad, India.

Booth, David, Jeremy Holland, Jesko Hentschel, Peter Lanjouw, and Alicia Herbert. 1998. *Participation and Combined Methods in African Poverty Assessment:Renewing the Agenda.* Department for

International Development (DFID), U.K.: Social Development Division and Africa Division.

Bradley, Christine, 1994. "Why Male Violence against Women is a Development Issue; Reflections from Papua New Guinea." In Miranda Davies, ed. *Women and Violence: Realities and Responses, Worldwide.* London: Zed Books.

Brunetti, Aymo, Gregory Kisunko, and Beatrice Weder. 1997. "Institutions in Transition: Reliability of Rules and Economic Performance in Former Socialist Countries." Policy Research Working Paper 1809. Washington, D.C.: World Bank.

Carvalho, Soniya, and Howard White, 1997, "Combining the Quantitative and Qualitative Approaches to Poverty Measurement and Analysis: The Practice and the Potential." Technical Paper 366. Washington, D.C.: World Bank.

Castellas, Manuel. 1997. *The Power of Identity.* Malden, Mass.: Blackwell Publishers.

Cernea, Michael. 1979, "Entry Points for Sociological Knowledge in the Project Cycle." Agricultural and Rural Development Department. Washington, D.C.: World Bank.

Cernea, Michael. ed. 1985. *Putting People First.* New York: Oxford University Press.

Cernea, Micheal, with the assistance of Apri Adams. 1994. "Sociology Anthropology and Development: An Annotated Bibliography of World Bank Publications 1975-1993." Environmentally and Sustainable Development Studies and Monograph Series 3. Washington, D.C.: World Bank.

Cernea, Michael, and Ayse Kudat, 1997. "Social Assessment for Better Development: Case Studies in Russia and Central Asia." Environmentally Sustainable Development Studies and Monography Series 16. Washington, D.C.: World Bank.

Chambers, Robert, 1989. "Editorial Introduction: Vulnerability, Coping and Policy." *IDS Bulletin* 20:1

Chambers, Robert, 1994. "The Origins and Practice of Participatory Rural Appraisal," *World Development* 22 (7). Wahington, D.C.: World Bank.

Chambers, Robert, 1997. "Whose Reality Counts?: Putting the First Last." London: Intermediate Technology Publications.

Chambliss, William J. 1999.*Poweer, Politics, and Crime.* Boulder, Colo.: Westview Press.

Charmes, Jacques. 1998. "Informal Sector, Poverty and Gender: A Review of Empirical Evidence." Contributed paper for *World Development Report 2000*. Washington , D.C.: World Bank. October.

Dahle, Cheryl. 1999. "Social Justice—Alan Khazei and Vanessa Kirsch." Fast Company, Issue 30, December 1999, www. fastcompany.com.

Dasgupta, Partha, and Ismail Serageldin. 1999. *Social Capital: A Multifaceted Perspective, Washington,* D.C.: World Bank.

Davies, Miranda, ed. 1994. *Women and Violence: Realities and Responses Worldwide*. London: Zed Books.

Dollar, David, and Roberta Gatti. 1995. "Gender Inequality, Income, and Growth: Are Good Times Good for Women?" Policy Research Report on Gender and Development, No. 1. Washington, D.C.: World Bank.

Economist Intelligence Unit. 1997. *Armenia Country Profile, 1996-97*. Lodon: The Economist Intelligence Unit, Ltd.

Edwards, Michael, and David Hulme, eds. 1992. *Marking a Difference: NGOs and Development in Changing World*. London Earthscan Publications

Edwards, Roberts, and Michael W. Foley. 1997. "Social Capital and the Political Economy of Our Discontent." *American Behavioural Scientist*, 40(5): 669-78.

Esman, Milton J., and Norman Uphoff, 1984. *Local Organisations: Intermediaries in Rural Development*, Ithaca, N.Y.: Cornell University Press.

Fajznlber, Pablo, David Lederman, and Norman Loayza . 1998. *What Causes Violent Crime?* Office of the Chief Economist, Latin Amercia and the Caribbean Region. Washington, D.C.: World Bank.

Floro, Maria Sagrario. 1995. " Economic Restructuring, Gender and the Allocation of Time." *World Development* 23: 1913-29, Washington, D.C.: World Bank.

Folbre, Nancy. 1991. "Women on Their Own: Global Patterns of Female Headship." In Rita S. Gallin, Anne Ferguson, and Janice Harper, eds. *The Women and International Development Annual*. Vol. 4. Boulder, Colo.:Westview Press.

Foley, Michael W., and Robert Edwards. 1996. "The Paradox of Civil Society." *Journal of Democracy* 7 (3): 38-52.

Foster, James, and Amartya Sen. 1997. "On Economic Inequality after a Quarter Century." 2nd ed. Oxford: Clarendon Press.

Fox, Jonathan. 1993. *The Politics of Food in Mexico: State Power and Social Mobilisation*. Ithaca: Cornell University Press.

Galtung, Johan. 1994.*Human Rights in Another Key*. Cambridge, U.K.: Policy Press.

Gelles, Richard J., and Murray Straus. 1998. *Intimate Violence*. New York: Simon and Schuster.

Giddens, Anthony, 1984. *The Constitution of Society*. Oxford: Blackwell.

Goetz, Anne Marie. 1998. "Women in Politics and Gender Equity on Policy: South Africa and Uganda." *Review of African Political Economy* 76: 241-62.

Greeley, Martin, 1994 "Measurement of Poverty and Poverty of Measurement." *IDS Bulletin* 25 (2).

Grootaert, Christiaan. 1998. "Social Capital: The Missing Link?" Social Capital Initiative Working Paper No. 3. Social Development Family. Washington, D.C.: World Bank.

Grootaert, Christiaan. 1999. "Social Capital, Household Welfare, and Poverty in Indonesia." Policy Reseach Working Paper 2148. Social Development Family Washington, D.C.; World Bank.

Grootaert, Christaan, and Deepa Naryan. 1999. "Local Institutions, Poverty and Household Welfare in Bolivia." Social Development Family, Environmentally and Socially Sustainable Development Network, Washington, D.C.: World Bank.

Holland, Jeremy, and James Blackburn, eds. 1998. *Whose Voice? Participatory Research and Policy Change*. London: Intermediate Technology Publications.

Hyden, Goran. 1997. "Civil Society, Social Capital, and Development: Dissection of a Complex Discourse." *Studies in "Comparative International Development* 32: 30-30.

Jackson, Cecile, 1996. "Rescuing Gender from the Poverty Trap" *World Development* 23: 489-504.

Jain, Devaki, 1996. "Panchayat Raj: Women Changing Governance." Gender in Development Programme. United Nations Development Programme, New York.

Kabeer, Naila. 1997. "Women, Wages and Intra-household Power Relations in Urban Bangladesh." *Development and Change* 28(2): 261-302.

Kabeer, Naila, and Ramya Subrahmanian. 1996. *Institutions, Relations and Outcomes: Framework and Tools for Gender-aware Planning*. University of Sussex; U.K.: Institute of Development Studies.

Kaufmann, Georgia. 1997. "Watching the Developers: A Partial Ethnogaphy." In R.D. Grillo and R.L. Stirrat, eds. *Discourses of Development; Anthropological Perspective*. Oxford: Berg Press.

Korten, David C. 1990. *Getting to the 21st Century: Voluntary Action and the Global Agenda*. West Hartford, Conn.: Kumarian Press.

Krishna, Anirudh, and Norman Uphoff. 1999. "Mapping and Measuring Social Capital: A Conceptual and Empirical Study of Collective Action for Conserving and Developing Watersheds in Rajasthan, India." Social Capital Initiative Working Paper No. 13. Washington, D.C.: World Bank.

Krishna, Anirudh, Norman Uphoff, and Milton J. Esman (eds). 1997. *Reasons for Hope: Instructive Experiences in Rural Development*. West Hartford, Conn.; Kumarian Press.

Leach, Melissa, Robin Mearns, and Ian Scoones. 1997. *Community-Based Sustainable Development: Consensus or Conflict?* University of Sussex, U.K.: Institute of Development Studies.

Lipton, Michael, and Martin Ravallion. 1995. "Poverty and Policy." In Jere Richard Behrman and Thirukodikaval Nilakanata Srinivasan, eds, *Hanbook of Development Economics*. Vol. 3. Amsterdam: Elsevier Press.

MacEwen Scott, Alision. 1995. "Informal Sector or Female Sector? Gender Bias in Urban Labour Market Models." In Diane Elson, ed., *Male Bias in the Development Process*. 2nd ed. Machester, U.K: Manchester University Press.

Marshall, Gordon. 1994. *The Concise Oxford Dictionary of Sociology* New York: Oxford University Press.

Max-Neef, Manfred. 1993. *Human Scale Development: Conception, Application, and Further Reflections*. London: Apex Press.

Milanovic, Branko. 1998. *Income, Inequality, and Poverty during the Transition from Planned to Market Economy*. Regional and Sectoral Studies. Washington, D.C.: World Bank.

Milimo, John T. 1995. "An Analysis of Qualitative information on Agriculture: from Beneficiary Assessments, Participatory Poverty Assessments and Other Studies, which used Qualitative Research Methods." Ministry of Agriculture, Food, and Fisheries. Lusaka, Zambia.

Moore, Mick, and James Putzel. "Thinking Strategically about Politics and Poverty." IDS Working Putzel. "Thinking Strategically about Politics and Poverty." IDS Working Paper 101, Univesity of Sussex, U.K: Institute of Development Studies.

Moser, Caroline, 1998. *The Asset-Vulnerability Framework: Reassessing Urban Poverty Reduction Strategies*. Washington, D.C.: World Bank.

Moser, Caroline, Annika Tornqvist, and Bernice van Bronkhorst. 1998. "Mainstreaming Gender and Development in the World Bank: Progress and Recommendation." Washington, D.C.: World Bank.

Narayan, Deepa, 1999. "Bonds and Bridges: Social Capital and Poverty." Policy Research Working Paper 2167. Policy Research Department. Washington, D.C.: World Bank.

Narayan, Deepa, and Katrinka Ebbe. 1997. "Design of Social Funds: Participation, Demand Orientation, and Local Organisational Capacity." Discussion Paper no. 375. Washington, D.C.: World Bank.

Narayan, Deepa, and Lant Pritchett. 1999. "Cents and Sociability: Household Income and Social Capital in Rural Tanzania." *Economic Development and Cultural Change* (47)4: 871-8.

Narayan, Deepa, and Lyra Srinivasan. 1994. *Participatory Development Tool Kit: Training Materials for Agencies and Communities*. Washington, D.C.: World Bank.

Narayan, Deepa, and Michael Cassidy. 1999. "A Dimensional Approach to Measuring Social Capital: Development and Validation of a Social Capital Inventory." Draft. Washington, D.C.: World Bank.

Narayan, Deepa, and Talat Shah. 2000. *Gender Inequity, Poverty, and Social Capital*. Policy Research Report on Gender Development, Working Paper Series, Washington, D.C.: World Bank.

North, Douglas. 1990. "Institutions and their Consequences for Economic Perfomance." In Karen Schweers Cook and Margarer Levi, eds. *The Limits of Rationality* Chicago, Ill. : University of Chicago.

Norton Andy, and Thomas Stephens. 1995. "Participation in Poverty Assessments." Social Development Papers 9. Washington, D.C.: World Bank.

Orbach, Susie. 1999. "Psychoanalysis and Social Policy." Seminar paper presented to the World Bank, Washington, D.C., April.

Patton, Michael Quinn. 1990. *Qualitaive Evaluation and Research Methods*. NewBury Park, Calif.: Sage Publications.

Portes, Alejandro. 1998. "Social Capital Its Origins and Applications in Modern Sociology." Annual Review of Sociology 22: 1.24.

Pottier, Johan, 1997. "Towards and Ethnography of Participatory Appraisal and Research ." In R.D. Grillo and R.L. Stirrat, eds.

Discourses of Devlopment: Athoropological Perspectives. Oxford, U.K.: Berg Press.

Putnam, Roberst, Robert Leonardi, and Raffella Y. Naetti. 1993. *Making Democracy Work: Civic Traditions in Modern Italy*. Princeton, N.J.: Princeton University Press.

Ravallion, Martin. 1995. "*China's Lagging Poor Areas.*" *American Economic Review, Papers and Procedures* 89. 301-5.

Ray, Raka, and Anna Kortweg. 1999. "Women's Movements in the Third World: Identity, Mobilisation and Autonomy." *Annual Review of Sociology* 25: 47-71

Rietbergen-McCracken, Jennifer, and Deepa Narayan. 1998. "Participatory Tools and Techniques: A Resource Kit for Participation and Social Assessment." Social Policy and Resettlement Division, Environment Department. Washington, D.C.: World Bank.

Robb, Caroline. 1999. "Can the Poor Influence Poverty? Particaptory Poverty Assessments in the Developing World." Washington, D.C.: World Bank.

Rodrik, Dani. 1998. "Globalisation, Social Conflict and Economic Growth." *World Economy* 21 (1): 43-58.

Rupesinghe, Kumar, and Marcial Rubio. 1994. *The Culture of Violence*. New York: United Nations Unversity Press.

Salmen, Lawrence. 1987. *Listen to the People*. New York: Oxford University Press.

Salmen, Lawrence. 1995. "Participatory Poverty Assessment: Incroporating Poor People's Perspectives into Poverty Assessment Work." Social Development Paper No. 11. Washington, D.C.: World Bank.

Salmen, Lawrence. 1998. "Toward a Listening Bank: A Review of Best Practices and the Efficacy of Beneficiary Assessment." Social Development Paper No. 23. Washinton, D.C.: World Bank.

Sartori, Giovanni, 1997. "Understanding Pluralism." *Journal of Democracy* 8 (4):58-69.

Schuler, Sidney Ruth, Syed M. Hashemi, and Shamsul Huda Badal. 1998. "Men's Violence against Women in Rural Bangladesh: Undermined or Exacerbated by Microcredit Programmes?" *Development in Practice* 8(2): 148-57.

Schwartz, S.H. 1994. "Are There Universal Aspects in the Structure and Contents of Human Values?" *Journal of Social Issue* 50 (4): 19-45.

Sen, Amartya K. 1981. *Poverty and Famines*. Oxford: Clarendon Press.

Sen, Amartya K. 1983. " Poor, Relatively Speaking." *Oxford Economic Papers* 35: 153-69. Reprinted in *Resources, Values and Development*.

Sen, Amartya K. 1984. "Rights and Capabillities." In Amartya K. Sen, ed., *Resources, Values and Development*. Oxford, U.K.: Blackwell.

Sen, Amartya K. 1985. "A Sociological Approach to the Measurement of Poverty: A Reply to Professor Peter Townsend." *Oxford Economic Papers 37: 669-76.*

Sen, Amartya K. 1992. *Inequality Reexamined*. Cambridge, Mass: Harvard University Press.

Sen, Amartya K. 1993. "Economic Regress: Concept and Features," *Proceedings of the World Bank Annual Conference on Development Economics*, 315-54.

Sen, Amartya K. 1997. *On Economic Inequality* 2nd ed. Oxford: Claredon Press.

Sen, Amartya K. 1999. *Development as Freedom*. New York: Knopf Press.

Shah, Shekhar. 1999. "Coping with National Disasters: the 1998 Floods in Bangladesh." Seminar paper presented in June to the World Bank, Washington, D.C.

Shapiro, Glibert, and John Markoff. 1997. " A Matter of Definition." In Carl W.Roberts, ed., *Text Analysis for the Social Sciences*. Mahwah, N.J. Lawerence Erlbaum Associates.

Silverman, David. 1993. *Interprettig Qualitative Data; Methods for Analyzing Talk, Text and Interaction*. Thousand Oaks, Calif.: Sage Publications.

Srinivas, Smita. 1999. *Social Protection for Women Workers in the Informal Economy*. Draft. Washington, D.C.: World Bank and Geneva: International Labour Office.

Standing, Guy, 1999. "Global Feminisation through Flexible Labro: A Theme Revisited." *World Development* 3 (27): 583-602.

Stone, P.J., D.C.Dunphy, M.S. Smith, and D.M. Ogilvie. 1966. *The General Inquirer: A compturre Approach to Content Analysis. Cambridge* MIT Press.

Strauss, Anselm L. 1987. *Qualitative Analysis for Social Scientists*. New York: Cambridge University Press.

Tarrow, Sidney. 1994. *Power in Movement; Social Movements, Collective Action and Politics*. Cambridge, U.K.: Cambridge University Press.

Tendler, Judith. 1997. *Good Government in the Tropics*. Baltimore, Md.: Johns Hopkins University Press.

Townsend, Peter. 1971. *The Concept of Poverty*. London: Heinemann Educational.

Tripp, Aili Mari. 1992. "The Impact of Crisis and Economic Reform on Women in Urban Tanzania." In Lourdes Beneria and Shelly Feldman, eds. *Unequal Burden: Economic Crises, Persistent Poverty, and Women's Work*, Boulder, Colo.: Westview Press.

Uphoff, Norman, 1986. *Local Institutional Development: An Analytical Sourcebook with Cases*. West Hartford, Conn.: Kumarian Press.

Uphoff, Norman, Milton J. Esman, and Anirudh Krishna. 1997. *Reasons for Success; Learning from Instructive Experiences in Rural Development*. West Harford, Con.: Kumarian Press.

Visaria, Leela. 1999. "Violence against Women in India: Evidence from Rural Gujarat." *In Domestic Violence in India: A Summary Report of Three Sutdies*. Washington, D.C.: International Center for Research on Women.

Weber, Robert Philip. 1990 Basic Content Analysis. 2d ed. Newbury Park, Calif.: Sage Publications.

WHO (World Health Organisation). 1997. *Violence against Women*. Geneva.

Woolcock, Michael. 1998. "Social Capital and Economic Development: Toward a Theoretical Synthesis and Policy Framework." *Theory and Society* 27(2); 151-208.

Woolcock, Michael, and Deepa Narayan. 2000. " Social Capital: Implications for Development Theory, Research, and Policy." *World Bank Research Observer* 15 (2), Washington, D.C.: World Bank.

World Bank. 1996a. *From Plan to Market: World Development Report 1996*. Washington, D.C.

World Bank. 1996b. *Sourcebook on Participation*. Washington, D.C.

World Bank. 1997a. *Poverty Assessment: A Process Review*. Operations Evaluation Department Document 15881. Washington, D.C.

World Bank. 1997b. *World Development Report 1997: The State in a Changing World*. New York: Oxford University Press (for the World Bank).

World Bank. 1998. *World Development Indicators*. Washington, D.C.

World Bank. 1999. *World Development Indicators*. Washington, D.C.

World Bank. 2000. *Poverty Trends and Voices of the Poor*. Poverty Reduction Group. Washington, D.C.

Wratten, Ellen. 1995. "Conceptualizing Urban Poverty." *Environment and Urbanisation* 7: 11-36.

[illegible] 19[illegible]. The Impact of [illegible] and Economic [illegible]. [illegible]

[illegible]

[illegible] West Hartford, Conn.: Kumarian Press.

[illegible]. Washington, D.C.: International Center for Research on Women.

[illegible]

[illegible]

[illegible] and Economic Development: Towards a [illegible] 27(3):15–27.

[illegible] Development [illegible]. Washington, D.C.: World Bank.

World Bank. [illegible] Washington, D.C.

[illegible] Washington, D.C.

[illegible]

[illegible]

[illegible]

[illegible] Washington, D.C.

[illegible]

[illegible]

Index

R